c

Plea
for
Liberty

Books by GEORGES BERNANOS
Star of Satan (Sous le Soleil de Satan)
The Crime (Un Crime)
Diary of a Country Priest (Journal D'un Curé de Campagne)
Diary of My Times (Les Grands Cimetières sous la Lune)
The Open Mind (Monsieur Ouine)

L'Imposture
La Joie
Jeanne, Relapse et Sainte
La Nouvelle Histoire de Mouchette
La Grande Peur des Bien-Pensants
Une Nuit
Scandale de la Verité
Saint Dominique
Nous Autres Français
Journal de Guerre

GEORGES BERNANOS

Plea
for
Liberty

DENNIS DOBSON

TRANSLATED FROM THE FRENCH

by

HARRY LORIN BINSSE

and

RUTH BETHELL

Translated from the French
by Harry Lorin Binsse and Ruth Bethell

Lettre aux Anglais—*Atlantica Editora, Brazil, 1942*
Plea for Liberty—*Pantheon Books, N. York, 1944*
First published in Great Britain 1945
Reprinted 1970
All Rights Reserved
Published by Dobson Books Ltd.
80 Kensington Church Street, London W.8.
Reproduced and printed by
Latimer Trend & Co. Ltd., Whitstable, Kent.

SBN 234 77643 9

C O N T E N T S

Preface

[7]

Letters to the English

[13]

Letter to the Americans

[89]

Letter to the Europeans

[119]

TO MY SON YVES
OF THE FREE FRENCH FORCES
BY WHOSE ACTION
THE WAR THEIR FATHERS BEGAN
WILL BE BROUGHT TO AN END
THE DEAD BE AVENGED
THE SHAM NEW ORDER BE OVERTHROWN
AND THE TRUE ORDER, FOUND IN HONOUR
LIVE AGAIN

PREFACE

SOME day it will perhaps be said that this book was written in exile; but for many months I have no longer felt an exile here.

However modestly and simply I may state this feeling, it would no doubt have been better still to keep it secret. I should be deeply ashamed to be taken for one of those wandering literary men who move on from one great city to another, and hand on heart, enounce, time and again, the same fatuous imbecillities. For me, Brazil is not a sumptuous, almost anonymous hotel, where I dump my bag until I can set sail for home ; it is my home, but I do not think I have earned the right to say so yet. I am too deeply in debt to deserve to be believed. I do not claim to know Brazil. I don't ; or not what the realists call knowing ; I mean, I have gradually lost the few notions I had which might once have given me the illusion of knowing. I know Brazil far less well than I did three years ago : but I feel I am beginning to understand it, and that is why I hesitate to speak of it to strangers, for by doing so I make known my debt of gratitude, and may appear to think I can thus acquit myself of it.

After Munich, I wrote that I had come to Brazil to live down my shame. This I have not done, I have found instead my lost pride, it is the people of this land who gave it back to me.

Perhaps this plain statement of fact should suffice. I fear to blur it by elaborating it. It is in any case intended only for the very few, who may well become fewer still. Though I hope to live long enough to see reparation made for certain acts of injustice—as men of law or churchmen make it, with indemnities, or processions—I do not believe that Honour is soon to be reinstated. The seed we have sown must first rot in the soil, before sprouting for a new springtime in new men's hearts. I shall not live to see this springtime.

It may be that my Brazilian friends will not see it either. What of that. We Frenchmen were not of the world we see crumbling about us. And you Brazilians were not of it either. In the necessarily makeshift world that will hurriedly be set up on the ruins of the other, we shall barely survive, you Brazilians, we French. But early or late, the quiet persistent endurance of man will live down the ages of Iron and Gold ; will refashion a life-size world ; and the world will be human again.

Patience, endurance : words that constantly occur in my books. Never do I write them but with tender recollection. Our people of France have had to suffer and endure, which is to say that they bore their suffering with decency, as though bred to it, and as a rule courteously. That is why, in spite of countless trials, they were supposed to be happy folk, as indeed they were, for they were in love with happiness. They liked to be happy themselves, and they were able also to enjoy the happiness of others. They sought it ardently, but prized almost as highly the desire and expectation of it.

Never would it have occurred to them to constrain it, or take it by force, snatching immediate enjoyment regardless of cost, at the risk of destroying precious seedlings and of making the future sterile : as does modern man. But the day will come when his civilisation will appear to be what it is : the removal by forceps of a still unquickened foetus : a monstrous operation for abortion.

Let me give an example. The people of France took 600 years to achieve national unity, and when in the XVIIth Century the master-piece was completed, it already belonged to us all, to be henceforth an imperishable portion of our universal inheritance. You and we together stand and confront those hastily improvised and violent nations which secrete power, or wealth, as a diabetic secretes sugar, or a man with dropsy, water, unaware that it is their own life's substance that is draining away. They consider themselves creators. They are wastrels. You it is who create, but they are in too much haste to see it. They seem to think creation can be set to any rhythm ; they mistake production for creation.

Whereas you create on a warp of time, they neither respect nor like time ; they barter it like any other goods. They know nothing of Patience and Endurance ; they will take no part in the great works of Life, no share in Patience ; they know nothing of how Life is all Patience and Endurance, and they despise your way of life because they are too crude to see in it more than a sort of indolent resignation. You appear to them to be unnecessarily slow in developing your land, by which they mean, refashioning it in their own image and likeness ; developing your land : meaning laying it bare, opening it wide to their exploitation. They can hear something stirring underground, they are not sure what it is, but they are absolutely determined to get at it at once, alive or dead. They measure the girth of your mountains, the pace of your rivers, the depth of your valleys ; they work out the cost in marks, florins, yens, rubles, piasters, pounds or dollars, of reducing all the obstacles, and bringing you welfare in the only form they know : wealth. They have forgotten one thing only : they may bore tunnels through mountains, dig new riverbeds, span or fill in valleys ; but no power on earth can change the nature of the people themselves, nor alter their deeply-held conception of traditional family life ; their idea, in fact, of happiness.

In Brazil, the calamity that my country has suffered has been felt as though it were your own. As indeed it was. I have never denied France's shortcomings, nor that she grievously failed the world. But when the modern world proclaims that it has been betrayed, the modern world is lying. We have never betrayed it. The world knew very well that thanks to it, our isolation was daily becoming more pronounced, and that in a state of society where economic autarchy lead inexorably to economic and spiritual autarchy, we were fore-

doomed to come to grief, because we were not understood and could
no longer love. They were all awaiting this downfall, some lamenting
a necessary and unavoidable sacrifice to the common good, others
bitterly triumphant that our turn had come at last. They awaited
that one slip that would leave the way clear. They long ago stopped
serving those historic human values which remain linked to our fame,
they were uncomfortably aware of their survival, and required merely
that we should renounce them to be wholly rid of them. And renounce
them we did. So implicitly that we produced momentary agreement
between foes at the point of re-engaging in mortal combat. We
renounced the old victory of France, and with it the principles for
which we fought and won. It is ourselves we renounced, by renouncing
our victory, do you see ? At the celebration of this solemn abjuration,
they were all present, friends and foes alike—remember ! remember !
there they all were, in seeming relief, unburdened, reconciled. For it
is Munich that saw our victory blotted out—not Bordeaux, not
Réthondes. And it took a Chamberlain, a man completely alien to
our nation, to believe for a single moment that, after betraying the
poor friend who had trusted us, we should not immediately do likewise
to the wealthy ally who, having egged us on to shame, had yet not
shared that shame. I was with you then, my friends. Your people
took the shock in silence, with a kind of tragic reserve, as though
dumbfounded. I see now that of all the nations of the world, yours is
doubtless the one we truly betrayed, and that the betrayal had gone
deep into your very soul. I am writing this not for you but for the
French who believe in me, and who know that I should not make
such a statement as this lightly. God forbid that we should pride
ourselves on what we have done to you, or crudely accept your hurt
as homage due to us, as a mere token of love ! A soul betrayed is
more than love betrayed : your faith in us once shaken, you could
lose faith in yourselves ; you were more hurt in your conscience than
in your feeling of friendship even. For your conscience and ours were
committed, I will not say to the same ideal, for the term is too vague
and abstract, but to a conception of life that was both spiritual and
carnal. You would not let yourselves condemn us, renounce us as we
had renounced ourselves ; yet you could not justify us without con-
ceding that such a conception of life was false, or that life had lied
to you.
  Life did not lie. We did that—once only in the whole course of
our history. But we shall make reparation for that day's lie, if need
be we shall wash away the shame of it in streams of blood. And should
we fail to do so, you yourselves would make reparation, in due course,
simply by carrying on your task, and going on living the life you
believe in, as we ourselves did for centuries. For that is the secret
of our greatness. While other nations strove to play their self-allotted
part, not the one for which they were fitted, but the one that gave
scope to their pride, or lust—Germany of the Holy Roman Empire,

Plantagenet England, Spain under Charles V—our true desire was
but to live in our own way in all security, to be what nature made of
us, or rather what it was daily making of us, for we tried to interfere
with it as little as possible. France was built up slowly—for we did
not expect to have room to make her bigger—solidly, because she was
built to suit our needs. She is just right for us, not too big : there
is no risk of her tumbling about our ears. To reach greatness, we went
the longest way round, but it was the only right way. We applied
ourselves to the task of becoming great without ceasing to be human,
I mean without rejecting the errors, mistakes, weaknesses, or even
absurdities which are more or less common to all mankind and keep
us in mind of what is and what is not humanly possible.

We hated supermen and superhuman things, we always held that
there was, between what was natural and what was supernatural, no
room for the superhuman. If now we seem to give in, it is because of
the desperate effort this diabolical counterfeit of the supernatural is
making, to gain supreme control of the conscience of mankind, and to
turn all his efforts war-wards, voidwards.

I do not at all suggest that your Brazilian ideal derives from France,
though some of your intellectuals would, too generously, have it so.
Moreover, in the last three years I have met few of your intellectuals,
living chiefly among your peasants. It is through your own peasant
that I came to understand your intellectual, and that is the plain
truth. I see now that your intellectuals were using French culture
to buttress themselves against a certain conception of life which the
people of your land reject instinctively : if it triumphed, it would
do more, they feel, than bring about their certain downfall : it would
dishonour and annul the work of the past, make nonsense of their hopes,
and compel them to admit, with their dying breath, that they had
nothing to leave posterity but illusions without substance, and that
it would be better had they never been born.

As your intellectuals see it, our culture is the most appropriate arm
for the common defence. But it is from their roots in the people of
the land that they hold their almost physical sense of imminent danger,
and the will to resist.

Since I have lived among you, my most moving experience, and
the one which doubtless brings me closest to your soul, is the gradual
daily discovery of how, in spite of appearances, sometimes unwittingly,
your most highly cultured social élite remains close to its peasant
origins in a thousand charming and significant ways ; which would
now only be true, alas, of a mere handful of the French aristocracy.

In fact your people know that they can hope for no good from the
superman, nor from his type of society. They are suspicious of the
superman, who is equally suspicious of them. How the supermen
would love to convict these people of indifference to progress, to shame
them out of their laziness, or their levity as they alternatively call it.
They understand perfectly well that we, by refusing to adopt the

particular rhythm which they wish to impose on human effort, do threaten to throw all their calculations out, in course of time ; for their wild rush of activity can neither turn aside nor slow down : it is a pouring torrent, a stone rolling downhill.

The world organisation they propose is a monstrous speculation on purely fictitious values, a bluff. It devours man's work, and then it devours man himself. So any real value, however small, once asserted or reinstated, is a threat to the whole system.

You are engaged in asserting such a value. Your coasts are so remote, your territory so vast, you are able to take your time, to work in tune with time, and to observe the laws of life. This is no cheap flattery. I am not claiming for your people that they know exactly what they are about, or what it is worth. Once they come to know clearly and distinctly what they are creating, the hardest part of their destiny will be accomplished. The great work happens within us first, almost unknown to us, through that inner power which seems to rise in answer to a silent call : this is the meaning—for nations as well as individual men—of the word vocation : *vocatus*, called. The call is not our responsibility, but to answer, or not to answer, is.

All these three years, friends, my family and I have shared the life of your peasants ; shared their toil and poverty, I had almost said. I have been profoundly glad to feel how your people are on the right track ; it has relieved and unburdened me, to see them carrying out their own appropriate task, not more, not less, in a world where most nations have learnt to despise theirs and envy others', and to get congresses of highly qualified experts to draw up programmes of so-called national aspirations. Your nation grows like a tree, like a poem, in accordance with an inner principle which the modern world fails utterly to understand, precisely because it has itself no inner principle : it tries to impose itself from outside, this monstrous but ephemeral victory over nature and man of human activity run riot : all dissipation and defiance.

Your nation grows without being conscious of it, as we ourselves grew in time gone by, which is much the best way of developing naturally, with no loss of right proportion or risk of becoming in course of time a giant's head on dwarf legs. Here, as once in Europe, man and the soil react upon each other, and each brings the other nearer perfection, locked in a relentless struggle the true nature of which has to be grasped. Here, man tames the wilderness by dint of sheer hard work, with his naked hands. The tinkers of mechanics may well laugh, the last laugh is not theirs. The cost may be in terms of long years, many dead : so is a great free nation made ; so does all the power and patience of the soil pass into the muscles and hearts of men.

The first time I crossed this land of rolling hills which stretches from Rio to the leafy capital of Minas, and still further, to the very edge of the vast dwarf forests of the Sertao, rising and falling like the waves of the sea in slow motion, I looked for something to remind me of my home villages; I saw mostly isolated houses, with uneven Indian cornfields full of weeds, wind-torn banana plantations, and bamboo plumes, proud and almost as empty as Claudel's great metaphors. Then the catch-phrase of the know-all ignoramus sprang to my lips: " They ought to . . . ", " Why don't they . . . ", " They might have . . . ", " They could . . . " But now at last I understand your peasants, so different from ours and yet so like them, for I was born to love them. To judge you by the work of your hands alone is a mistake and a contradiction. In my country the soil is friendly to man. Yours is not inimical, but it is unresponsive. Your peasants and their families live lonely and poor, with no villages, no neighbours. It might be possible with one well-directed blow to shatter the resistance of your soil and rip it open. For that you need merely the necessary material, technical skill and hard cash. But then your soil would no longer be yours. It is now your means of achieving freedom, it would become the instrument of your enslavement. The foreigner, comparing you to your European counterpart, says you do not work it hard enough. Perhaps your work is less, your toll of death is more than theirs. They give the sweat of their brow, you give your life. What you snatch from the soil, by cunning rather than by sheer strength, is barely enough to keep body and soul together; and your small homes, so touching, so peaceful in the evening light, seen from a distance, are more like the rafts of the Carribean fishermen in their perilous insecurity. If you appear to us to husband your energies, it is because you have none to spare. You use them to the best of your ability, applying them wherever danger threatens, and some you keep for song and dance and music-making; for experience taught you long ago that your powers of resistance lay not in your guts or your muscles, but in your nervous system, like animals in the natural state, and women, and artists. So your output of energy cannot be measured with ours, yours has kept a quality which ours has lost. You are therefore able to suffer and endure where others would quickly lose heart. This is not only the secret of your power, it is the secret of your incomparable resignation too. For once the rhythm of your life is broken, you die immediately, naturally; and you die without regret, for it never occurs to you to try to defend your patient, ingenious lives for one hour too long, against those hostile powers which you know are still beyond control.

But listen, before you are the masters, before you conquer hunger, thirst, fever, the poisonous herbs that grow in your soil more readily than the health-giving kind, the plagues of insects; long before you lose that (in no way servile) deference to facts, you will have given the world an infinitely more precious treasure than pastures and orchards : a free people, a people bred to freedom.

CRUZ DES ALMAS,

15th January, 1942.   Barbacena, Brazil.

Letters to the English

O MEN of England! These pages will reach you, I suppose, some
time next December. Christmas is the feast of childhood. I call
down the blessings of childhood on the English nation. Hurrah for
your childhood! Unfortunately, we French have never taken much
pains to understand the English. In the fifteenth century our ancestors
called them " Godons " and followed them in the streets with cries
of " Ware tail! " because they thought that, as a punishment for their
sins, they carried this devilish appendage hidden in their breeches. We
never understood you English very well, though many of us did know,
even then, that English children are among the loveliest in the world.
A happy Christmas, then, to the children of England! We thought
of you all as " milords " with high collars and fat paunches, as men
enjoying huge fortunes derived from cotton mills and West Indian
sugar, as the people who had invented the pound sterling, the race-
horse, and—one day, when you were feeling particularly liverish as a
result of eating boiled mutton floating in a melancholy sea of potatoes—
the umbrella. And now, for the last six months, day after day, you
have been telling us a fairy-tale, a tale that no serious adult, no man
of ability or experience, could possibly understand—a children's tale.
Hurrah for you English children!

No one knows better than I do that, in the course of centuries, all
the great stories of the world end by becoming children's tales. But
this particular one has started its life as such, has become a children's
tale on the very threshold of its existence. I mean that we can recognise
in it the threefold visible sign of its destiny. It has deceived the
anticipation of the wise, it has made the faint-hearted eat humble-pie,
it has staggered the nitwits. Last June, all these folk, from one end
of the world to the other, no matter what the colour of their skins,
were shaking their heads. Never had they been so old, never had
they been so proud of being old. All the figures that they had swallowed in the course of their miserable lives, as a safeguard against the
highly improbable activity of their emotions, had choked their arteries,
and they were stuffed tight with statistics. They were ready to prove
that with the Armistice of Réthondes the war had become a mathematical impossibility ; as though man had been made for mathematics
and not mathematics for man. Some chuckled with satisfaction at
the thought, but they were not the most dangerous, because hatred
is a salt which has the property of preserving old men from corruption,
at least for a moment. Others threatened us with the contagion of

their pity, dissolving before our eyes, melting into impotent, vile-smelling tears. " Alone against the world," they said. " It is a children's story." And that is precisely what it was—a tale for children. Hurrah for the children of England !

Men of England, you are now writing what public speakers like to describe as one of the great pages of history. I should like to say it more simply, in simpler words. But there are no simple words left, just as there is no honest bread. Well then, if the best words have really got worn out, we must make others ; we must make words of freedom for free men ! At this moment you English *are* writing one of the great pages of history, and I am sure that when you started, you meant it as a fairy tale for children. " Once upon a time, there was a little island, and in that island there was a great people up in arms against the world . . ." With such an opening as that, what old fox of politics and business would not have shrugged his shoulders and closed the book ? Your victory is a child's dream made real by grown men.

To all you who may read this book in six weeks or six months, or perhaps never—for who can foresee the fate of these modest pages across so many miles of sea ?—I wish you a merry Christmas. I am trying to wish it with joy in my heart, because joy is a debt that the whole world owes you. Of what use would our sorrow be to you ? What good has sorrow done anyone ? The only genuine sorrow is born of shame : shame alone is sorrowful because there is no cure for it. It is the only human evil from which death offers no hope of deliverance. I have not accepted shame, why then should I accept sorrow ? Let it be enough that I accept disaster. May its whole weight weigh upon us. May it crush us alone. Night has truly fallen on my country. It may be that I shall never see the end of it, but night holds no terror for me. I know that by marching right through the night we come to another dawn. Whether or not I shall experience it in my own person is now of little importance. The great thing of my life has been not to see but to believe. What we see is but lent to us, what we believe is given to us forever. By faith alone I can possess. What has my own poor experience taught me of my country ? Little enough. A few living men, many of whom are now dead. A few shreds and tatters of history which have escaped the gnawing teeth of rats, or of cads—a thousand times more destructive than rats. Some landscapes—intransmissable scenes which will die with me.

In many ways my country remains for me a mystery, the clue to which lies deep within myself. May it remain there ! There are lesser peoples—the Italians for instance—petty, envious, ill-conditioned races, who find in scorn and hatred a necessary tonic, who seek end-lessly to impose themselves on others, though in their hearts they know that, try as they will to find it, they have no real identity. My race is too old and too illustrious to feel the need of imposing itself. It has but to state its name. I bear its name, the name it gave me. Not like a feather in a hat, not like gold lace upon a sleeve, not like some upstart title. I neither earned it nor paid money for it. It is not something apart from me. We are one. I try to bear that name, as I bear the name of Catholic, with due humility, that is to say, naturally : as naturally and as simply as I can. To be humble does not mean to seek occasions of humiliation. To seek such occasions is dangerous and prideful. It is enough to be oneself, neither more nor less in the sight of God. I must not be turned aside from my goal by the thought of what the name of France meant in the days before I was born, of what it will mean in days to come, of what it means for others now. When I shall have laboured stubbornly to the end, then perhaps it will be given to me to understand better. Then perhaps I shall see, having first believed. Like all those of my country who went ahead of me from this world, I shall know what France is only in the next ; but before my small task is finished and I go to join them, I shall most certainly have discovered what a Frenchman really is.

I must apologise for writing so confidentially. Truth to tell, it is the only way I know. I did not start writing until I was over forty, and the extreme kindness which the public has shown me for eleven years still does not make me feel like a professional writer. Whatever my work is worth, it is not a well-run stage where I try to provide entertainment, or, in other words, try to earn my daily bread. My work is myself, it is me at home. I speak to you, pipe in mouth, my jacket still damp from the last shower, my boots steaming in front of the fire. I do not even trouble to go into another room to talk to you. I do my writing in the living-room, on the table at which, later on, I shall be having supper with my wife and children. There is no library for introducing me to you in the usual way for I have no books at all. Nothing lies between us but this penny notebook. Lies are not written in penny notebooks. I can offer you nothing but the truth at that price. If you think I am being too familiar with you, remember that I am a man who awaits rehabilitation only from a future which he may never know, and can therefore speak as one already dead. I say rehabilitation, not victory. For victory is in *your* hands, but the rehabilitation for which I look is in the tiny fists of the children, those in the cradle who care as yet neither for you nor for me, those who may not yet be born. Not the redressal for which my country looked after 1870 ; not revenge on the enemy. It is France of tomorrow redressing France of today, the rehabilitation of father by son. Affronted, but not defeated, is our generation. There is something to be said for wiping us out altogether, us and the affront we suffered, so we should be forgotten together. That is impossible. But we can at any rate see to it that our sons do not, out of consideration for us, bewail this affront as a calamity. It is a calamity, but they must not know it as such, they must not feel pity for us, or the day may come when, out of pity for themselves, they too will give up the fight. Let

the French take heart : the open wound must heal, the scar grow hard
as stone.

   This is not written in bitterness or revolt, but from a mind deeply
at peace. And though it is written for you, I am not sure you will
understand me in England ; but as a nation you know when silence is
best : I can trust you not to offend me with condolences. And I
really prefer not to be understood too quickly, not to hope at all for
understanding : I know no better way of being understood in the long
run. I want to tell you as sincerely and plainly as I can what an old
cripple of the last war, a Frenchman, is thinking, in solitude and
exile. I am not speaking, hand on heart, in the name of France, as
from a political platform. No one ever had the right to speak in the
name of France except its saints and heroes. And they spared their
words for deeds. I do not claim I can make you understand France.
I am not sure I understand her myself. I am not trying, she gives me
no time, she sweeps along on this great adventure that has neither
beginning nor end, being spiritual ; a spiritual adventure undertaken
by more than usually realistic and carnal men. This contradiction is
our weakness and our strength : this paradox is our history. If we
stopped to consider it too long, we should get no further. We know
this contradiction is at the root of all our disasters, but it can be
resolved only by going ahead, or others maybe will settle it for us. We
are a Christendom on the march, and that is what the world will not
admit, because it gets on so much faster than we do—but its goal is
different. We are a Christendom on the march. We know very well,
in spite of boasting and flattery at home and abroad, that it is no
trumpet-led triumphal march past. Look at our history, it is one
long tale of patience and endurance. No nation has more patiently
welded its destiny, put its land together, put its mistakes and follies
right. We are a nation of peasants and artisans, working all out, six
days a week. But people only give us a glance on the seventh day,
when we contentedly put on our Sunday best, fill our glasses, and go
dancing with the girls. We are a Christendom on the march towards
the Kingdom of God, but not empty-handed. We should never have
planned so long a journey, there's plenty to do at home : but it happens
that God in his goodness has appointed us to carry liberty, equality,
fraternity to all those other nations whose place on the map we are
so vague about ; and so off we go, ready to save the world . . . On
condition, of course, that we can save with it our own fields, homesteads,
beasts, not forgetting the small savings the notary looks after for us.
   We are a Christendom on the march, on foot, you understand,
dragging along great clumsy loads of household stock, for we are
attached to our little all, and want to leave none of it behind. We are
a Christendom marching to a kingdom of equality, liberty, fraternity,
which we don't always find it easy to believe in, because we believe
most easily what we can see with our own eyes, and that we have never

seen. Lord, then, we're not going fast. There's no hurry, we must spare the shoe leather, with cobbling so dear nowadays. There are always some bright lads who go prancing up and down the line, laughing with the girls, and who come a cropper, still laughing. We love them, we are proud of them, we recognise their likeness to us, that part of us that comes awake each time we have a glass too many. They may be good riders, they won't reach the stopping place before we do. And all down the centuries, we have, daily, dimly, to repair their repeated daredevilries. They got themselves beaten at Agincourt and Crecy. They once spent any amount of our money on conquering the Kingdom of Naples, moonstruck by the beauty of the girls ; and they brought back nothing but debts and the " Naples disease." They charge the enemy with a great flourish, and come back sometimes as swiftly as they went. So our history looks frivolous, while none is in fact more serious, more moving, more human. Because of these silly boys, careering backwards and forwards, we appear not to be advancing. And when they come tearing round us again, everyone supposes that we have given ground. True, we move slowly, but were we suddenly to stop, the world would notice, its heart would fail it.

Once more, I do not expect such words to be understood in these days, and when the time of understanding comes, they will long have been forgotten. I apologise if they appear presumptuous, they are not : in these shameful days the last thing I feel capable of is lying to myself. When I say the world's heart will fail it, I do not mean it will cease beating, though I believe the modern world capable of living without a heart. We are no better and no worse than the rest. True, we do not hide our vices, our Christianity is the least pharisaical in the world, but they scandalise far less than our absurdities. The most constantly recurring of these is the ever-ready ear we lend to the plea for pleasure-giving. We do try to please, the better to conceal a much deeper feeling, for the truth is we long, above all, to be loved : too much to confess it, too much to succeed. We end by claiming boldly that it is so, believing it ; showing ourselves now tender, now cynical, now sincere, now bragging. Therefore the world mistrusts us, mistrusts that small glowing hearth we tend down the centuries ; though hardly an ember show red among the ash, still, it suspects, the earth might yet be set ablaze. We alone of all nations have made ourselves utterly at home in the New Testament, belonging wholly to the New Law. We practised power in our day, we inspired fear. But it immediately became urgent that fear should give place to love. To win love we have spent more heroism and folly than the gain of ten empires would have cost. But courage fails at the last, we see our goal slip out of our hold again, and again we fall back on our raging desire to please. For lack of better means, we try to please by pushing into the limelight spinners of phrases, and pedants, dancers, singers, brainless blond moustachioed 2nd Lieutenants, aged Célimènes, no less out-moded petty bourgeois demagogues. When our supply runs short, the foreigner makes his own puppets : the recipe he has from us. This is how the 1914 Poilu came into being, that hero of Variety, sentimental, tongue-in-cheek, front-line practical-joker. Whereas in fact we make war in good honest fashion, humbly, stubbornly, just as one makes a good honest living for one's family. And it is our living which we won from them that they have trampled in the mud.

We shall not gather it up again. Perhaps I met some of my English readers between Loos and Vimy, or much later, in that black bitter March on the fearful empty gaping roads of Albert and Montdidier. We are still the same men, to you I can speak what I feel. I will not gather up this living they have thrown away. My old hands will not touch such bread, no fold of my army coat, that kept the smell of the dead so long, shall wipe it clean. I will not eat again of the bread the Old Man of the Armistice once shared with me. I am an exile from my country, I can also be an exile from our one-time victory. I left my country two years ago, in that other sinister autumn, on the eve of Munich ; for though a free man could still live there, he could not breathe freely nor live honourably. I mean, a free man can survive under organised tyranny, because the element of risk adds nobility to his life. But there was no risk in the isolation to which a Frenchman was already condemned in 1938 : merely crushing humiliation. There was no enemy, and the enemy was everywhere. Treason was nameless, featureless, yet French opinion was undermined on all sectors, in all departments, the very nerve-centres of the French people were ignominiously tapped. Almost wholly intent on its earnings, the Press was carrying on noisily, only the better to hide the terrifying silence of a nation that had lost faith in itself and was slowly falling apart. In such circumstances, though freedom still figured in the written law, to men it had no meaning, their minds were blank. Free speech fell back like a bird trying to fly in the void.

I left my country, too proud to take without giving, and giving had become impossible. I left without knowing for certain in which of the Americas I would make a new home, nor how I would feed my family. My one wish was to live down my shame in some forgotten corner of those boundless lands. Since coming here, I have not been seen in the gilded cities on the coast, I have not lived the life of a literary playboy on a lecture tour ; I have not lined my exile's nest, nor have I displayed my unhappiness to the public gaze. When, one day in June, the news of our dishonour reached me, I was very far west, beyond the last railway station, beyond the reach of rail or road, in the heart of the Brazilian *sertao*, that land of dwarfed and stunted forest where the only paths are those made by wild cattle. In that country there is no such thing as dining out, but a man has time to question his conscience and to listen to the answers that it gives. Our little wireless set, run off a battery so old that no one knew its age, and impossible to protect from the ravages of ants as big as wasps, was constantly interrupted by shrill and melancholy whinings like those of a dog tormented by fleas. The daily storm beat against the earthen walls of our house, and struck with a heavy, ominous sound upon its thatched roof. Outside, in the " corral ", the tree trunks shone red in the rain. We were all standing round the ridiculous contraption that looked so like a broken-winded toad, for all the world as though it had been the grotesque and formless image of our despair.

You in England wonder how we are to be saved. The answer will not come from that accessible side of us, which everyone knows or claims to know. The light-hearted, merry-making soul of France symbolised by the Gallic cock cannot give it. The cock is a stupid bird, it is absurd to make it the emblem of a nation whose arms from time immemorial bore three fleurs de lys on an azure field. Our calamities do not harden us, we are never more human than when suffering : this is the secret of our unflinching weakness, by this we survive. Listening to our hideous mechanical lung croaking out the death sentence of our one-time victory, I had no memory of its ever having belonged to me at all, and the thought that relieved my heartache was this : that we had nothing left. We were the generation of full graveyards and empty hands. We are supposed to be a proud nation, we are really humble and fervent, knowing how night repairs the damage of the day, day repairs the night's, and the sins of one day are forgiven by the time dawn breaks on the next. I am trying so hard to speak to you in England in the name of what our kings used so pleasantly to call " the small people ", " la menue gent ", because to them the proudest of us, however high his birth, turns back, when all else fails, as to his childhood's home, as to childhood itself.

Of longer lineage than any of our great families, they are more noble than the nobles, alone noble, in fact, among the upstarts disguised as their betters. They have picked up some of the vices of the successful bourgeoisie, but their hearts have remained clean. They see this bourgeoisie bears no trace of the old token sign of lordship, and no power in the world will make them bend before these arrogant, rabbit-hearted masters, who look down on them and fear them both at once. You may reply that the masters they chose for themselves were still more unworthy. But the demagogic politicians would not have the power they have, were they merely exploiting their poverty : they exalt their pride, they treat them like kings. To every king his courtiers, flatterers and fools. They are accused of being revolutionary, as though one could expect a nation to become conservative, that is static, when it has faults to mend all along the line, and can mend them only by keeping going ; a nation of labourers, sowing seed relentlessly for a thousand years, and when the last sheaf is gathered in, it drinks to next year's harvest. Nothing will ever stop the forward march of such a nation, its hope shall not be broken, its courage will not fail it, for hope and courage are one and the same. Notwithstanding our admirers, this courage of ours is not so much elegant as stubborn.

It is not a weapon so much as a tool—a well-worn tool.   Oh, I know,
we have had our Bouvines, our Fontenoy, our Valmy, but they were no
more than episodes, pretty pictures in a book, flowers in a field, and
it is not the flowers in the field that count.   One does not look to
the poppy and the cornflower for grain.   No, but the people of
France, with that homely tool of theirs, their simple courage, have
triumphed over every ordeal.   They wore down the Hundred Years
War ; they wore down the heresy of Luther ; they wore down the
fanaticism of Spain, that bloodstained clerical monarchy which put
the gibbet in the place of the Cross, and tomorrow they will wear down
our shame.   Not only will they avenge it, they will wear it down.   They
will wear down those responsible for our shame, shame itself will be
worn away.   They will do it in their own good time, day by day, for
they never go back on a job once done, but wonder each evening, in all
simplicity, how to get through tomorrow's.   " Is this the end,
Mother ? " little St. Theresa of Lisieux asked the Prioress on her death
bed.   " How shall I die ?   I shall never know how to die . . . "   It is
such words as these, not high flown words from Plutarch's Lives, that
rally our people to their colours in every age.

   Not to understand that is never to know us.   What has that little
Carmelite to do with the colours of France ?   If it comes to that, what
have three pure lilies on an azure field to do with the oldest fighting
nation of Europe ?   Who can say why it is that the Romans make us
yawn ?   Why are the hairy giants who make the hearts of young
Germans beat so fast, to us but heavy, awkward louts ?   The Romans
seem always to be posing for their statues, and even if it is true that
they are demigods, why can't they leave us in peace ?   They despise
life, we love it dearly, to us it is so beautiful, so sweet.   How dare they
take leave of it so coldly, as though it were a mere stranger.   As to the
Germans, why are they always rolling ferocious eyes, and drinking beer
out of skulls ?   Why do they scorn death, which is even cruder than
scorning life ?   If their hatred of their enemy is such that they long
to slake their thirst from his skull, where is the merit in attacking him,
since they go into battle drunk ?   To die drunk is the worst disgrace
that a man can know.   None can claim the name of hero who has not
shown his mettle at the sacred threshold and crossed it with calm and
seemly gait.   And if he cannot do that, he had far better weep openly
like a man, and not go about roaring and foaming like a beast, for life
is worth weeping for . . .   " How shall I die ?   I shall never know
how to die."   So must Jeanne d'Arc have thought, on the morning of
the 30th May, 1429.   What we find so touching in that childish cry
is precisely that it holds no scorn of death.   Rather it welcomes death
with a careful courtesy, a sort of quiet shyness, a fear of offending it.
It is the sign by which we recognise the fulfillment, the completion,
the perfection of the kind of heroism whose servants and witnesses in
this world we more or less consciously know ourselves to be.   What

matter that it is a child's cry ?   Such childish words it is that rally the men of France.

A great French writer who unfortunately is descended from inferior Arabic or Levantine stock, M. Charles Maurras, grew indignant on one occasion over the fact that the young people of France, though they take a ready pride in the victories of their country, seem to have a sentimental predilection for tales of heroes in defeat, where all is lost save honour.   This view he regarded as a monstrous perversion, not (as no doubt he imagined) on logical grounds, but as a direct result of his own racial inheritance.   For him the word " victory " connotes pillage, loot, and captured women exposed naked in the market-place. Young Frenchmen do not prefer defeat to victory.   But they make no mistake in holding that a hero is never more great than in the hour of disaster, and that war would be mere bloody slaughter if it did not sometimes raise man above himself to martyrdom.   Our one popular epic, the Song of Roland, is a story of defeat.   It is this child of France, defeated, dying, with his face to the enemy, one hand raised to Heaven, the other humbly seeking his friend, who has stirred the hearts of boys and girls of my nation for ten centuries.   Such is the unerring choice of French honour.

I am speaking to you from the depths of a double exile.   The immense expanse of sea which separates me from my country can always be crossed.   The immovable obstacle in my way is the memory of that indignity.   Indeed, today, I could not write down the name of any of our historic defeats without shame, for only the one which now weighs on us shows everything lost.   Is my testimony the less valid for being made in the very presence of ignominy, beneath its very gaze, as it were ?   I make no god of Honour, certainly not a French god.   Honour has kept men company through the ages, it may have been an angel once, no one can tell now ; it has shared our poor life so long, in the end it has grown like us, it sins as we do—but a sinner can be redeemed. French honour is a Christian Honour ; baptised into the Church, it has forgotten that, centuries ago, it was but a bloodstained idol.   True, it is not wholly blameless.   It has on its conscience looted cities, raped women, cellars of wine drunk dry.   It can echo the words of La Hire to his confessor : " I have done all that men commonly do in war," and for these faults the comfortable conformers, Scribes and Pharisees, look at it askance.   But though possessed at times by the spirit of violence, it has not wholly forgotten its baptism : the lustral water, the white robe, and the words of pardon.   There is more humility in honour than in many of the wealthy parishioners who take the front seats in Church. " Oh, come," you may say.   " Whoever heard of honour being humble ? "   It is so, and so were its origins, for it was no gift of kings, it arose from among the people themselves, with the days of chivalry. It flowered on the simple courage of the people like a crimson rose on an old thorn bush.   The heroes themselves set the standard.   What could our moralists, our theologians, our professors of psychology say to it ? The heroes are its guarantee. They were neither giants nor supermen, nor Judges of Israel, but very human men, so human that we think of them as people on our own level, neighbours, friends we can talk to. They never considered themselves heroes or saints, though often they were both. The greatest amongst them still come to us carrying their crowns of glory in their hands, wearing their ordinary, everyday clothes, anxious not to intimidate the little boys of France. Before ever we knew the word Honour, or before we could spell it, they were already part of our childhood and that is where they belong. We have seen St. Louis, sword in hand, confronting the Saracens upon the beach at Damietta, but we have seen him too, dying in sackcloth and ashes for the remission of his sins. We know that he never turned his back upon a living foe, but we know, too, that he put water in his wine —yes, water in his wine, as a penance, and that he and his gentle little wife trod very warily when Blanche of Castille, that most unaccommodating of mothers, was about. We have seen Jeanne d'Arc at the storming of Les Tourelles, but we have seen her too, as old Lord of Gamaches saw her once, falling from the Curtain Wall with an arrow in her breast, dragging down ten foemen with her, while he hurled himself forward in her defence, old warrior that he was, grasping his double handed axe. But we have seen her again, as you English saw her, among the Bishops and men of law at her trial in Rouen, her poor cheeks hollow with fever, the sweat standing out on her obstinate little face, her mouth trembling, when in the stifling air of the audience chamber, after days and days of bullying, she suddenly gave up the struggle, tendered her sacred word and her sworn oath, fair flower of chivalry! " If you do that wicked thing to me " she cried, " harm will come to you, body or soul." What a cry of distress, a sweet childish cry ! Oh, to kiss the air through which it rang, that innocent cry, to which, till the end of time, the furious barking of the guns of France will give answer ! Who could ever doubt of our honour, when, for one short moment, the incarnate Lily of the royal standard, the shining sword of France, our national Saint, so mistrusted herself ?

Today you see us as you saw her then. We have denied our Voices. " By St. Catherine and St. Margaret, God has communicated to me His great pity for this treason to which I gave consent when, to save my life, I abjured the truth and made recantation. He tells me that to save my life I have risked damnation. If I said God did not send me, I should be damned, for God did truly send me. My voices have told me that in admitting that I acted wrongly I have committed a grave fault. What I said, I said from fear of the fire . . . " It is true that we have denied our Voices. It is true that we have betrayed ourselves. But remember this, the girl who after long exhausting cross-examination, weak and uncertain, went back on her word, or had it snatched from her weak grasp, was the same girl who, some weeks before, had rejected the offer of ransom made her by John of Luxembourg.

" In God's name, you are making a fool of me ! I know that the English will kill me, thinking after my death to possess the Kingdom of France. But with a hundred thousand more Godons than there are, they will never conquer it." We have denied our voices, and each of us may believe, as Jeanne herself believed, that it was from fear of the fire. But she feared neither steel nor fire, nor any danger of this world, until the doctors and casuists had succeeded in troubling her conscience. It was doubt, and not fear of the fire, that overcame her. No blow from the enemy would have shaken her, but she bowed before " her reverend Fathers in God." Our nation's lot is much the same, its conscience has been tampered with and betrayed, and those who betrayed it were those who claimed the right to be its guides. It is true that it denied itself, but not until those guides had first, themselves, denied it.

I wish to be its witness. I cannot claim to belong to the people, as our demagogic politicians do ; that is why I may know them better than they know themselves. My feelings are unlike those of the section of the bourgeoisie which alternately exploits and sentimentalises. The name " bourgeoisie " carries no weight, as far as I am concerned ; in our country, it stands for a certain attitude, that is, a certain small set of prejudices and habits, many of them quite respectable, but with no intrinsic connection with our traditions and our past. There was once a real French bourgeoisie. It was that Third Estate so well described, a hundred and fifty years ago, in the words of Siéyès. " What " he asked, " is the Third Estate ?—nothing. What might it be ?—everything." Everything is what it became in fact. It destroyed our monarchy, it broke down the time-honoured structure of our society, it absorbed or corrupted that small nobility of land and arms whose poverty it disdained, not realising that by doing so it was striking a fatal blow, not at a few decent, harmless folk who had stirred it to envy, but at the military and peasant tradition which had made our nation great. It laid hands on the domain of France and mortgaged it at far more than its true value, in order to transform it in accordance with its own tastes ; and it died of its own victory. Today, the French bourgeoisie is merely a medley of turncoats, cursing the class from which they sprang.

The Bourgeoisie despises the people, but it fears them. I blame it less for its scorn than for its fear. The people will not be treated as enemies of the nation. The trouble with French bourgeoisie today is that while it is rich and powerful enough to render useful service to the community, its origins are too base for it to rise to a conception of disinterested service, one that doesn't pay. It makes a great to-do about all the precious " values " which it sets out to defend, always naïvely using the possessive pronoun. It says OUR Law and Order, OUR Property, OUR Justice. To protect the people against its claims is to be a traitor to the country. To stand up for the people is

to stoop to flattery, but it is a great honour to become, by flattery,
the champion of the bourgeoisie. Because I write as I do, the intellectuals in the pay of the bourgeoisie try to make out that I am a
demagogue. In fact, I am a man of Old France, or rather, of France ;
for a thousand years of history are not to be wiped out by a hundred
and fifty years of wretched fumbling. Old France is still alive and
whole in the France of today. Anyone with good will can see it. I
can see it. I rate the people neither above nor below their true value.
I consider that I owe certain duties and enjoy certain privileges. Such
as they are, it is only decent that I should use them in the service of
those who do not share them. It is, in any case, rather pointless to
talk of privileges today. " *There are no more privileges—there are
only duties.*" That was the ruling principle of the French popular
monarchy, which still claims my loyalty.

I know as well as anyone the faults and errors of the French, but
no consideration, whether of persons, parties or class, shall keep me
from stating that the people of France were not primarily responsible
for the disaster which has overcome my country. Nothing shall keep
me from denouncing the fatal breach which, after 1918, separated the
mass of the French nation and its privileged few, nor from insisting
that the people were not the authors of this breach. I accuse the
privileged classes of France of having betrayed the people by making
them doubt themselves and the things they loved. I do not say that
this act of betrayal was always consciously performed : the privileged
classes of France, in order to justify their incapacity to fulfil the
promises made at the time of the last war to organise peace, and to
see this great task through whatever the cost to themselves, have,
since 1925, adopted towards the rest of the nation an attitude of
perpetual fault-finding, backstairs defeatism, and even cynical con-
tempt. The people of France believed themselves to be fighting for
Right, Justice and Universal Peace. The men they were prepared to
respect for their greater education and culture laughed in their faces
and said " Nonsense " to these great words. Having failed to get
anything out of the war, they gave out that war was a fraud, and the
people sadly wondered why these gentlemen had once urged them on
to it. They thought that they had been fighting for Democracy,
and the intellectuals scathingly rejected this dowdy, out-of-date
novelty. These intellectuals, eaten up with pride and impotence,
lacked the humanity to understand, or even to try to understand,
what it was that the people meant by their simple use of the word. It
did not occur to them that the illusions of a great people are precious
and fragile things, or that by using a knife on them, they were running
the risk of destroying the very root of their hope. In their blind
egotism, these wretches tortured the conscience of our people by
overwhelming them with ironical questions to which they had no
answer. Finding no guiding thread through subtle and contradictory
explanations, they gave up the whole game. In their anger, they

attacked, not the men who had failed to give them Right, Justice and Universal Peace, but the ideas themselves, which they proceeded to regard as ridiculous and Utopian conceptions. The idea behind the League of Nations was fine and appropriate, and wholly in accordance with our old Christian tradition, but those who wanted to put it into practice—if they ever really wanted to—were impotent. It was not them, however, that the people derided, but the idea itself. The abject conspiracy against the soul of my country, against its faith and its hope, against, one might say, its innocence and purity, has just been dramatically underlined by the solemn substitution of the new slogan : " Work, Family and Country," for the ancient formula : " Liberty, Equality, Fraternity "—as though one was a contradiction of the other.

When the judges of Jeanne d'Arc decided her cause was to be lost, they determined that she should incriminate herself. They had made her swear that she would give up wearing men's clothes. Then, during the night, they removed her woman's clothes, and compelled her to dress as a man. Then they accused her of perjury. Something similar has happened to the French people. They were robbed of their illusions, their hopes, the humble devoted humanitarianism which sustained them all through the last century : an ideology which, no doubt, contained many errors, but which long use was rendering harmless, and which would at long last have been assimilated by their age-old traditions for what it was worth. Then, deprived of all that had kept their hearts warm, shivering with cold, they slipped over their shoulders the woollen jacket of the Popular Front, and their ears were deafened by all the hypocrites shouting shame on them. The term Bolshevik was deliberately and disingenuously fastened on a people which, from 1914 to 1918, had given evidence of an extraordinary power of discipline and heroic unselfishness. In order to get away with the job of breaking up national unity in the interests of Messrs. Mussolini and Hitler, they accused the people of wanton destructiveness.

As long as ten years ago, I denounced the privileged classes of France for refusing to shoulder their responsibilities. I call this treason, because up to the very last day, the day of the final surrender, they went on speaking the language of honour. And now cowardice is called moderation, wisdom, prudence, though cowardice is the one fatal risk, the only irreparable improvidence. They dubbed themselves " preservers " and, indeed, the word is truer of them than of most people, truer than it has ever been before, since they " preserved " what they have preserved for the enemy. They " preserved " an empire for him to devour at his ease later on. Even so, that is not the worst of their betrayals. I accuse them of undertaking in the interests of the enemy a " spiritual revival " which they were too unskilled or too cowardly to undertake in actual fact, when it was still a practicable possibility. They stood before the people with the scandalous intention of restoring Work, Family and Religion, before first restoring Honour. They put themselves forward as Doctors in Christian ethics. They preach contrition with no intention of amendment, absolution without restitution or reparation. They respect the Letter and betray the Spirit. What do I care what names they give themselves, even when those names are the ones I am myself proud to bear ? I know that salvation will never come from them. If they had won in the fifteenth century, I should have been English, in the sixteenth, Spanish. If they won to-day, I should become a German. When, on February 23rd, 1429, young Jeanne set out with Jean de Metz and Bertrand de Poulengy on the first stage of her journey to Chinon, the privileged classes had already thrown in their lot with the enemy, acquiescing in the New Order, the new Europe, the " Lebensraum" of Plantagenet England. The most junior student of theology would have found it child's play to prove, in a series of impeccable syllogisms, that it was to the interest of God, The Church, all upright folk and every sound principle, to come to terms with the conqueror. But, heaven be thanked, neither Jeanne nor the people of France have any skill for argument with casuists. And so, sooner or later, there comes a day when they hear, in the silence of their hearts, the Saints of their country speaking to .them.

March, 1941.

I am all the more ready to write to you again, English friends, in that this letter, like the other, is but a random message, cast into a future I shall not know, cast into the future as though to the wind and the waves. For if I believed that I could reach the ears of living Englishmen to-day, I should certainly not be so ridiculous as to try to correspond with a whole nation, I should not burden the reader with so futile a job. But a day will come, I know,. when some young man of your country, one doubtless still unborn, will happen upon these dead pages, and his glance will bring them back to life because they will have touched his heart.

O, Englishmen ! We have all sinned against childhood ; we have created a mean and savage world, dry and cold, where the genius of childhood can yield neither its flower nor its fruit, a world where childhood is impotent and old age monstrously active and fertile. Do not take our misfortune lightly : shameful and pitiful as it is, it may one day be the fate of the whole of mankind : world-chastisement for all-pervading error. We are not a hyprocritical people : we do not try to hide our miseries. All have betrayed childhood. But they exploit its holy insignia, they call themselves young, they speak in the name of the youth. Who would now dare look German childhood in the eye, that stunted mockery ? What has Mussolini done to

Italian youth ? And as for the children of Spain, for six years they have lapped fresh blood out of their saucers, they have had Torquemada as wet-nurse, they have from birth suckled at his black breasts. Yes, all have betrayed childhood, but we, at least, did it openly. France has publicly bestowed herself upon the old, upon old age, upon the spirit of old age ; the most youthful, the most laughter-loving nation of the world has, through despair, cast herself into the arms of old age, as though she no longer thought herself worthy of any other sort of death. The Old Man considers himself her Master, and history will show that he has been tricked and bound by his youth-ful prey. In him is incarnate the shame which, at the peak of its distress, youth dared not take upon itself. It put all its shame onto this Old Man as oil is poured into a goatskin bottle, and one day, at the first favourable turn of fate, youth will cast into oblivion Shame and the Old Man together.

Do not be surprised at such words, in England. In Marshal Pétain you see merely an old gentleman of nearly ninety, and for old gentlemen who reach a record age you have the same kindly admiration you have for any other winners, and that respectful, almost filial tenderness which you likewise feel for ancient inns and patriarchal trees. But do not summarily judge our old men by your own ! The only course open to a Frenchman is to remain young all his life. Those of us who grow old do it badly, for they age too soon. They start growing old, take on old age, and pride themselves on being old, at a time when your men are still working, to keep up appearances or because they must, then throwing off work for play just as once they cleared the classroom desks to rush out to football or cricket. Our race grows old badly, for the simple reason that God has marked it with the sign of youth ; it cannot grow old without denying itself, it ages like a man recanting. We supply the world with the meanest, craftiest, most virulent specimens of old age because in France old age is above all an attitude of mind, an acceptance ; it is a deep-laid scheme, a self-imposed discipline and a revolting sort of asceticism. It is a career on which a man embarks as early as possible ; a system and a religion. I told you before that the French Bourgeois, in the course of two centuries, has grown into a type of man altogether different from the national type, but you certainly did not believe me, and to-day, you still do not believe me. You think that our bourgeoisie, like yours, is legitimately descended from the bourgeoisie of old, where-as in fact ours swallowed up the old one just as it swallowed up all the institutions of the Monarchy. Even if I produced proofs, I should get no further towards convincing you ; you would tell me that these ancient quarrels interest no one, and that wherever it came from, in two centuries our middle class has had every chance to engraft itself on the nation. And so it has ; but this is of more concern to you, in England : two centuries were none too long a time for it to build up a tradition and impose upon the rest of France a new conception of

French life suited to its own peculiar interests and prestige. And I say this is of more concern to you English, because it is in the name of this special morality that men sought to justify the Armistice, and to-morrow will justify the French withdrawal.

I do not really mind whether these words shock you or not; your people are shocked at many things, and that is why they avoid mentioning them. My people name them outright, and as soon as that is done, they no longer fear them, for they have made them powerless. I say that there is but one shocking thing for a man of my nation, and that is not to understand. As long as you have not honestly striven to understand the disaster of my country, you will remain unjust, and if you think you can be quits with the oldest nation in Europe, by decently averting your eyes from her distress, as though it were a shameful, " improper " sight, you will commit even greater injustice, which sooner or later shall be expiated.

Men of England, we were together at Munich! We let you down, but two years earlier, we, together, let the world down. We betrayed you, but we had already been traitors together at Geneva, Shanghai, Barcelona, Prague and Tirana. The world was full of our words of honour thrown into the dustbin before they had served any purpose. The history we have written together since the 1918 Armistice, with the blood of five million men, is not of a kind for children to read. If they understood what it really means, the well-springs of happiness might dry up within them, their youth might wither away. It is realistic history, I mean history made by seasoned men, so seasoned that they yield to your finger like an overripe pear. You may retort that it did not sap the courage of your own heroic boys nor their readiness to face death. It did not sap the readiness of ours to die, it undermined their will to live. It is not the same thing. It made them disgusted with themselves. What Englishman, since God created Englishmen, has ever felt disgusted with himself? Nothing can make you disgusted with yourselves, because your attention is distracted from your earliest infancy: games, animals, nature, and a simple and practical moral code designed for immediate application, as ready to the hand as a familiar stick. To be at one with your conscience, all you need to do is go to the club together, read the same papers, drink the same tea, enjoy the same games, and stick to the same subjects of conversation, strictly selected with the idea of avoiding controversy, for you do not wish one to undertake to convince the other at all. What does Munich matter to you, now? And those " guilty men " you have indicted in a book? Their mistakes or their crimes do not concern you, and you will pay no heed to them. In an Empire where order must be maintained at all cost, there is no room for either regrets or remorse ; the imperial highways must be kept clear. We French are not on such polite terms with our conscience : we do not sleep apart, only meeting at an impeccably served breakfast or luncheon, we are a couple holding all things in common, for better or for worse ; hateful to our neighbours with our shouting, fault-finding, laughing, tearful, disorderly ways. Hearts are tempered or broken by such prodigious confusion. the very confusion of love itself. Alas, I fear such words will not make you think any better of us, for you value nothing more highly than what you call " savoir-vivre ", and it is true that we do not know how to live, we have never had time to learn how to live ; on the contrary, it is from life itself that we are learning all the time, with a sort of burning and consuming joy of which we ease ourselves in laughter ; for we used to laugh as no people laughed before, and no one knew the secret of our laughter ; it was a very shout of freedom, it was a shout of faith in man to which mankind was well advised to stop its ears, for had it one day broken out freely, it would have rung louder than all the Marseillaises in the world. But what is the point of talking of our laughter in a world so narrow, hard, compressed ; a world of iron soldered with gold at every joint, at which God himself will not laugh before the fullness of time.

Men of England ! We together are responsible for this world we have made. We were the two richest and most powerful nations of Europe, we were the two outstanding scions of Christendom. We had our full share of heroes, saints and martyrs, and scattered about in their hundreds, kneeling cathedrals with arms upraised and hands joined, so clear and pure that even their shadows hallowed the land. From the thirteenth century onwards, we were ready to give the nations justice and peace. Why did we exhaust ourselves in fratricidal strife ? At the moment when preferment-selling Italy, rotten under its jewels and brocades, was making the Holy City a den of thieves and a cistern of iniquity, you turned your back on the Church instead of helping us to save her ; you gave your faith to the first Hitler. At the same time, through your defection, the Church only narrowly escaped bondage to another kind of monster : Spanish clerical dictatorship, the Black Terror, with all the cruelty and sordidness of Hell. It offered the hatred of man in homage to God made Man, and the blood of the sinner in the ineffable chalice, in place of the blood of the Redeeming Lamb ; and Christ was subject once again to the yoke of the Old Law. For three centuries now, the policy of our two countries has never been inspired by a common ideal : we allowed the united front of Christendom to be broken and we lost the sense of European unity, the foundation of which had been so well and truly laid by the genius of the twelfth century ; we pursued the will-o'-the-wisp of an empiric equilibrium, in the hope of being the sole beneficiaries of its instabilities. We let the Christian front be broken, and religious hatreds, the pride and cupidity of rival churches and the fanaticism of the pious all united to carry to the highest level of malificence the schemings of Machiavellism borrowed from the gangsters of the

Italian Renaissance. We meddled in your revolutions, you meddled in ours ; not a wound was sustained in either country into which we did not astutely pour boiling oil and melted lead. But what is the point in digging up the distant past ? It is no longer recognizable to-day, although it is there, alas ! It is there, to the last jot or tittle, for we cannot be quit of our mistakes.

I want to speak of something much nearer us, if I can. God knows, I should have preferred to say nothing to-day about our one time victory ; I scarcely dare write its name—yet that name is everyones and has been used by everyone ; our victory no longer has a name. What of it ? Perhaps we once gave it a name together, only I fear it was not the right one, the one chosen in their hearts by the now forgotten dead. I have just thought of something. All our military cemeteries are in the hands of the enemy. I have never thought of it until now. So we have not two million prisoners, but four, and that is no joke. I should not let myself speak of our one time victory, if, though we won it together, I believed it really belonged to both of us ; but this I have never believed. Of course, we paid the same price for it, blood and tears. But I wonder if it ever had the same meaning, in your minds and ours. To-day you know what it is to fight for your land and hearth and home. This war is your war. We pretend to share the other one with you, our old comrades ; yet at heart we were sure that it was only ours : our war, the war of the lads of France, against professional soldiers, men of the trade who thought themselves better than the rest of us ; it was a pose, they really thought they could put it over us, and, by God, it was up to us to show them real men . . . Make no mistake, I am speaking in their name ; I apologise for talking their language as though I had a right to it and enough simplicity of heart for it. At least I did serve with them, in the same ranks ; the lowest ranks. They did me the honour of living and dying at my side—not under my orders. They treated me as equal to equal, we drank from the same tin mug—Oh, how deeply I loved them ! You English, with your snug uniforms, your polished belts, your odd sportsmanlike knapsacks and diminutive cigars, were taken by our lads for rich men's sons, " milords ", people from the big house who condescended to come out and lend a hand at the harvest ; and if you warmed their girls for them, they were rather proud of it. Good God, I fear you will think all this very vulgar indeed. You did not hear, as I did, along the Peronne road, what the common labourer from Aubervilliers said ; sallow-faced, hollow-chested, black with filth and powder, his shoulder torn on a machine gun tripod. His voice was hoarse, he spat a great gob of fresh blood and said, seeing your beautiful Scotch troops stretched out on the grass, " What a damn shame to have such big strapping fellows kick the bucket ! " And as I looked at him, he added kindly, to reassure me, " Don't worry ! It's only my throat ; my lung box is O.K." I had never seen him before and I never saw him again.

Yes, that war was their war, and don't take me for a demagogue. I am fully aware what all of you have done to the word whose Greek root is " demos." Lightly come, lightly go, as the saying is, and it is fitting that such words, invented by vulgarians, should be of use only to liars. It is precisely because I am neither a democrat nor a demagogue that I have the right to speak honourably about the people of my country. I do not doubt that an American patriot, for instance, can love his people as much as I love mine, but for him there is no mystery involved. However proud one may be of Brooklyn Bridge, still one could not pretend to have for that technical masterpiece the feeling which Chartres Cathedral inspires in me. The French people is not merely the body of manual labour of every stock and origin from which the middle class recruit their chosen few. It is that, of course, but much more. It is old France still alive before my eyes ; it is the priceless instrument, the precious human material out of which our kings gradually fashioned my country ; it is old France herself, I tell you, even to her very faults ; and I honour her as such, for her faults are in fact those of the unworthy masters who seek to make use of her. The only excuse for a rider thrown by his horse is that he was riding a treacherous beast ; now if this nation were vicious at heart, how could the Monarchy and it together have made such magnanimous history ?

That war was its war. For the sake of propaganda, professional men of letters had invented the term, " Prussian Militarism " ; and the French people took it up, for lack of better, but its meaning in their hands changed completely. That was its war. What on earth could a worker from Birmingham or Manchester, a miner from Wales, a fisherman from Yarmouth, or a farmer from Yorkshire think of that war ? . . . I suspect that none of them thought very much of it, except to see the empire threatened, the sea routes endangered, and every Englishman affected both in his interests and in his dignity as an Englishman. They would have thought it a good idea to let the Navy deal with the mess single-handed. The principle of conscription is a shock to a man's conscience. But since it had to be, they got on with it, it was His Majesty's good pleasure. There we see the reasoning of a wealthy nation sure of the permanence of its parliamentary institutions, the soundness of the pound sterling, and God's favour. But the trouble was that our people were not at all sure of its institutions or of its bankers or, even less, of God's favour. For a hundred years and more, our people had distractedly wondered who had got anything out of their famous revolutions, and whether they had really freed the world as the demagogues kept telling them. That the demagogues exaggerated a little our people admitted readily, for they are not so easily taken in : they treat this species of men with the same hearty good humour, absolutely devoid of respect, as they show, for instance, to street walkers. Granted that the world is not yet set free ! But that the French people had been given the mission of hurling tyrants from their pedestals—this they never doubted for an instant ; it is written in History, sung in the Marseillaise ; on this matter anyhow the demagogues were not lying.   The sad thing is that there are tyrants everywhere, not to mention those who spring up again on the very spot where others have been knocked down.   The bourgeois blamed the aristocrat ; the unbeliever blamed the priest ; the priest, the unbeliever ; and whatever one does, there are always starving widows, motherless children, bailiffs to sell the furniture of the poor.

Injustice is everywhere to be seen, and our nation is too old a nation, a people too burdened with experiences not to admit of injustice as one admits of sickness, ugliness, death.   Only this is not the whole story : our people noticed long ago that some injustice is superfluous, senseless, of no use to anyone, not even to those who use it, and since they imagine they no longer believe in the Devil, they are inclined to think that somewhere in the world must be found the shady den where, through stupidity or malice, plots are thus gratuitously made against the peace of the human race.   Victor Hugo accused the Kings and the Priests, but there are very fine priests in the working-class parishes ; there are even good kings too, good czars whom we go in family parties to welcome at the Bois de Boulogne Station ...   How can one make you understand, in England, this nation given over, for a hundred and fifty years, not to party strife—for our parties are not organised like yours— but to that confusion of party programmes, formulae, ephemeral groupings, of which self-seeking petty intellectuals are always ready to take advantage ?   Among these political imposters were our hypo- crites of the Right, furious at the revulsion produced, not (as they would like people to think) by their principles, but by their persons ; and assuming then, as now, the utter demoralisation of our people. Whereas, though exploiters of men's conscience are as common as flies among us, it is because the French conscience affords them healthy and nourishing food, for good sentiments yield a better return than bad, and if goodness of heart is perhaps less easy to exploit than selfish- ness or hatred, the gain is twice as great.   Parasites of social justice batten only on high-grade consciences ; they soon starve to death on dessicated or corrupt consciences.   France in 1914 was neither dessic- cated nor corrupt.' She felt cheated—cheated but not taken in ; cheated, or rather betrayed, or rather hoaxed ; hoaxed, in the name of her own principles and immortal slogan, in a world not dedicated to Liberty, Equality, Fraternity, but to Money and Profit.   Cheated, betrayed, hoaxed even in the admiration which this world continued to give out of sheer habit, an admiration she felt was unreal, and of which she perceived the irony.   But where did the betrayal come from ? Where was the Traitor ?   Who was cunningly turning men's hearts against her ...   Then, one evening, they read in the papers, over their apéritif, that the Emperor William had declared war on them in the name of Prussian Militarism, in order to do away with the French Revolution once and for all.

That war was their war. But our Peace has not been their Peace.
That was their war and they waged it as they did everything else,
with the same cynical diligence and passion for finished, abiding work ;
finished in its slightest detail, perfect in what you can see and even
more perfect—if possible—in what you do not see, or what will be
noticed only by a fellow craftsman. That war was theirs and they
waged it with love. How well I know I shall not be understood in
England ! They loved their war and they had no doubts about it.
I should never have dared to tell them so face to face, but I say it now :
I tell the secret which they never trusted to me, but which shone out
of them and lit up the humility of their lives, their death-throes, their
death. If you point out that the survivors will read these lines without
understanding them either, I shall reply that their testimony is ir-
relevant, because they are not the same men, they have not survived
their own greatness ; and whoever helped them to survive ? They
fought the war with love, they loved it. Now I beg you not to quote
me as saying, as the newspapers used to do, that they refused to take
sick-leave in order to get back quickly to the trenches : they took all
the leave due to them ; they even invented a variety of tricks to lengthen
it on the quiet. They loved the war and they cursed it, as they instinctively loved any work which required all the skill and patience
of their hands and arms ; they loved it as a weaver loves the fine fabric
which wears out his eyesight, as the glass-blower loves the hollow stem
which wears out his breath, as a navvy loves a firm, springy soil,
where every stroke of the pickaxe makes the handle sting. That war
was theirs because they found its pace slow enough to suit them,
because it wore out the patience of the dabblers, because it was a
workman's job, a skilled job, well within their scope. They had their
own language for it. They said " We'll stick it, we'll get them," as
though they were speaking of loosening steel beams or tearing up a
stubborn root. That war was their war : not that they took it up
fully consenting, or that they turned up an hour ahead of their time ;
but the thing was settled, they carefully weighed the pros and cons,
reckoned the cost, totted up the risk involved, and once all that was
set in order inside their great heads, they didn't give a damn for what
the popular papers and the soap-box orators had to say. A few months
earlier, the bulk of them were protesting against military slavery,
against the brutality of the officers, against armaments ; and they were
perfectly capable of getting themselves killed for nothing, to annoy
a sergeant major, to startle a friend or because of a bet made at the pub.
They all firmly believed that they didn't give a damn for glory. They
were waging war against war, that is how they saw it. They were
settling an old score with war, they were proving that conscientious
citizens, emancipated lads, can get rid of war. And then they gradually
came to love this war of theirs, because they had taken it out of the
hands of the military men and won it from them ; they had got a firm
hold of that lovely, passionate creature, which for centuries had served

the pleasure of the despots ; she was going to scratch and bite, but they were getting her with child all the same ; men would say of them afterwards—for they had no hope of surviving the nuptials—those were the fellows who begot upon war a victory such as has never been seen : an anti-military victory, a kind of innocent victory, a victory conceived without sin.   You understand, of course, that this imagery is mine and mine only, and that I invented it for you and for you alone. As for the men I am talking about, they would merely have smiled : " What the devil are you getting at ? " they would have said, " it's much simpler than that."   That is as far as they could get and their " much simpler " thing, deeply hidden in their good honest hearts, they did not know until death revealed it to them.   I am sorry, I owe you an apology for speaking so long about the past.   But I have to make you understand how so much honour was lost, how so much honour was lost.   And if it is not enough to say that our peace dis-appointed the world, we must find out what sort of men were let down by it.

I realise I am talking a lot about the last war, but as I see it there is only one war : it has lasted a quarter of a century.   You English embarked on a new war, when you resolved to make a stand alone in your island fortress or to be buried beneath its ruins.   But at that moment we were out of action.   But listen to me : without the popular, revolutionary victory of the Marne, the moral rout of the French élites which so appalled you in 1940 would have come about twenty-eight years earlier, after Charleroi, when a Government very like the one which foundered in June, 1940 had also fled to Bordeaux, and was making ready to declare Paris an open city against the will of Galliéni. The leader of the French bourgeoisie was at that time called Caillaux, and he resembled Paul Reynaud like a brother.   So the drama of the Armistice already had its actors and its audience, and it would have developed to its conclusion, to the final scene, to Marshal Pétain's capitulation ; which is, in fact, not Marshal Pétain's, but the prerogative of a certain category of men to which he belongs, whose spiritual chief he had aspired to be, and of whom he is now the symbol.   I once again apologise for calling this class of Frenchmen the Bourgeoisie.   I do not at all mean what the Marxists mean ; even less do I wish to give the word a general, universal value.   There exists, indeed, a bourgeois spirit, common to all the bourgeois classes in the world, but in which they participate in unequal measure ; so I shall only speak of ours, or rather a section of ours—whether large or small makes no difference— which, although for more than half a century kept out of power, or only wielding it indirectly (by means of politicians controlled by it who at the same time repudiate it in public as it is detested by the mass of voters), nonetheless had succeeded little by little in pushing its creatures into the best and choicest positions in the government, in journalism, in the Church, in the Academies, whereby it lays claim to guide the conscience of the middle class and all decent, orderly men perturbed by threats of revolution. I am not confusing this part of the bourgeoisie with the bourgeoisie itself; I merely say that it has become the élite and directs the bourgeois conscience. Is this clear? If you cannot admit this, it will be quite impossible for you to understand the Armistice at all, or its moral causes. Never forget that in 1914 as in 1940, the men I am speaking of would gladly have sacrificed greatness to security and have devised a peaceful, reactionary, rural France, where they could have hoped to live quietly at last, out of reach of upheavals. " You don't mean the men we saw treating defeated Germany so ruthlessly ? " you will say. You would come nearer the truth if you said that they were ruthless in their search for security ; then they hoped to find it at Germany's expense ; now they think they can find it at France's—there is the whole story. In those days they would have sacrificed Germany, Europe, the whole world for the sake of security, just as today they sacrificed France, the honour and greatness of France. They are not aware of doing wrong. They do not understand greatness as we do, you and I. When they say that happiness lies in mediocrity, they are far from saying it with the smiling and whimsical irony of a Horace : they are expressing a whole philosophy of life, that of Comfort. For a French bourgeois will rarely admit that he is rich : he is " comfortable ", he " lives in comfort". These people would like France to be comfortable too, to take her ease, to stop striving after greatness and notions of greatness, for the word always rings in their ears like revolution, a promise of revolution. They would like France to resemble themselves, so as to call themselves " France." And France won't. Unhappily for them, France never would. For fifty years, as they say, France has voted Left. They went as far left as they could. But France always went a little more left still. And they could not see that it was to spite them, out of revulsion for their persons. They took her to be frivolous, irresponsible, proud, self-satisfied and spoilt, and concluded according to the honoured precepts of bourgeois education that France needed to be put through the mill, and that a bit of real trouble would soon bring her to her senses. Then France would be theirs again and they could talk to her reasonably, and the little homily they had up their sleeves is the one you hear today. Marshal Pétain is merely the instrument which spouts it into the microphone. The homily was ready, and how they longed to preach it ! To them, the 1914 war was to have been a penitential war, a war of expiation, like that of 1870, which, for however short an interval, brought into power the Right-Minded people, the National Assembly, the landed proprietors, Marshal MacMahon . . . and suddenly down over the heads of the old men with their bald domes and wavering toothless gums, down on these sermonisers and smooth tongues, came crashing through the whole height of our French firmament—the white lightning of the Marne !

The battle of the Marne warded off the blow of the Armistice and the Bordeaux homily for a quarter of a century.   And it is our people who won it, who snatched it away from under the very noses and beards of our sermonisers and smooth tongues.   I say our people, though it is true that all took their share ; for there are popular victories, like Bouvines and Valmy, and there are military victories like Austerlitz ; and here at Verdun, for instance, our people held on patiently, dully, almost hopelessly, holding for the sake of holding.   But at the Marne they rose, they rushed to the Marne as though to the barricades.   Not to vindicate their country so much as themselves, to vindicate their honour as men.   The day before, they might have accepted anything.   Then, suddenly, they were aware of the insolent, scornful pitying stare of the men opposite, the professional soldiers and be-monocled officers, and they had that rush of blood to head and heart, that rain of blood on the eyes, that uprush of popular rage : " Ready ? Forward march ! " and they marched forward.

This is not a mere exercise in fine writing.   If you misunderstand our people and suppose it to be what the bourgeois élites would have it, you will have nothing to say to such a victory and its causes. The Right-thinking people have called it a miracle, not out of deference, but literally, for lack of a better word.   Everything is a miracle, everything is by the grace of God, I am Christian enough to know that. There is the miracle, here is its instrument, a more or less conscious, more or less worthy instrument, but always chosen, *vocatus*, called. There is the lifting of the siege of Orleans, and here is Jeanne d'Arc. There is the Marne and the people of France, hard-headed, tender-hearted, people with powerful hands.   That these people who voted wrong should have been even for a moment the instrument of Providence was as difficult for the Pharisees to admit as for the Sorbonne men and the opulent prelates of the Rouen tribunal to admit the intimacy with God of an illiterate peasant girl who was so immodest as to wear men's clothing.   I have told you this many times, and I do not mind whether I am believed today or not ; I shall continue to bear witness for my crushed, humiliated people as they would expect of me, were they still capable of expecting anything.   The people I have been speaking of did not really want our one-time victory, and they did not like it.   The man who did want it with all the strength of his heart, yearning for it from the depths of his soul, was Georges Clémenceau, and he was not one of them ; he scorned them : he died hating them.   Then, as now, the French bourgeoisie had on its mind only revolution and a threat of revolution ; its sense of social status was already stronger than its patriotism.   When it fought anti-patriotism and anti-militarism, it was not so much serving militarism and patriotism, as using them for its own ends, linking their cause to its own, their prestige to its prestige.   It was for the same reason that it became clerical. Of course, such scheming is never more than half-conscious, not even deserving to be called scheming ; we should see it rather as a mere reflex of the instinct of self-preservation. By preserving themselves, these élites would preserve everything they represent, but they never question whether they are still élites, that is, whether they carry out the function of an élite. Nor shall I ever tire of driving home this capital point. A society in which prestige no longer corresponds to services rendered, where the governing classes receive more from the community than they give, is a society on the high road to ruin. In 1914 as in 1939, our bourgeoisie went to war as though it were some silly adventure, of which the bourgeois economists had demonstrated the mathematical absurdity before the event. Then Jaurès and the Socialists were the pacifists : it was Jaurès who wanted Franco-German collaboration, and who inveighed against England and Russia. In 1939 the situation was reversed, and the bourgeoisie quite naturally took the opposite side to the English.

No war is possible without an ideal, and it was the people, not the bourgeoisie, which gave the 1914 war its ideal : it was ultimately against German nationalism and militarism that our men rose. It is too often forgotten, especially abroad, that this 1914 war was the first in which our French bourgeoisie really participated, serving fully in all ranks, even the lowest. The War of 1870 was still a war of professional soldiers, and those admirable Paris shopkeepers who took their turn standing guard on the fortifications during the Siege, swathed in shawls and mufflers, visited daily by their wives, were less the forerunners of the heroes of Verdun than the reincarnation of their forebears of the *Ligue*, caricatured for all time in one of the greatest books of our literature : *la Satire Ménippée*. The whole of French military history was wrought by the nobles and the people. Even in the days of Molière, a bourgeois soldier would have seemed almost as laughable as a bourgeois gentleman. Granted, the grandsons of the national guardsmen of 1870 gave proof, forty years later, that the traditional dislike of their class for the profession of arms was not due to cowardice. But none the less, perhaps unconsciously, they kept in the trenches a sense of heroic sacrifice of class, not unlike that of a sister of charity or a missionary choosing to share the life of the poor or the natives. In the mud of Massiges or Craonne, they were make-believe beggars among the real beggars : they had not exchanged one form of destitution for a worse one, but bourgeois comfort for destitution beyond belief. They were probably not sufficiently aware that if their sacrifice was greater, they also had more to defend : they knew the value of the stakes, whereas the ordinary poor devil had nothing to lose, since he possessed nothing, not even a clear notion of what, after all, belongs to all : tradition, culture, the spirit . . . If such an opinion were uttered in their presence, they were horrified. War ought to be waged by the rich, said some. By the poor, thought the

others . . . At my age, with my eldest son fighting for us overseas,
surely I can try to make everyone agree : war, alas, should be fought by
the old !

The bourgeoisie had no ideal, and it could not have any, for it
respects the letter but knows nothing of the spirit. For all its practical
positive sense, it has never bothered to create a morality for its own
particular use, though its own bourgeois professors have often worked
out such systems for it. But it mistrusts novelties ; it likes sturdy
tools which have already given sound service. Whenever a pressing
need arises in the moral sphere, it borrows what it wants from Christianity, no more no less ; by which I mean that it turns to the clergy,
confident of not being put off with inferior goods. Its only way of
idealising war is to see in it, like the clergy, an expiation. But it at
once gives this word a practical, positive meaning : expiation like that
of an insolvent debtor, or of the spendthrift in the hands of his creditors.
Not being in anyone's debt, as it supposes, guardian and living symbol
of Order and Property as it is, such trials could befall only the enemies
of Order, Property, Society, meaning its own enemies. Thus, courage-
ously, heroically participating in the war of 1914, it constantly foreswore
that war's spirit. Even when, for purposes of propaganda, it published
in its newspapers our famous slogan : " war to end war ! " the phrase
made it smile, but it was a wry and angry smile. Not that it liked the
war, but it detested even more what it called utopias, will-o'-the-wisps,
or whatever can arouse the imagination of the popular masses and
give them the idea that the established order is not established forever.
The poor devils conscientiously made war on war, and the bourgeoisie
muttered in its beard, with unwitting ferocity, " you'll wake up, you'll
get over it ", a precept with which it imbues its own sons, scoffing at all
their dreams.

War once over, why did common sense not come back into its own ?
Clémenceau the indomitable had been relegated to his Vendéan cottage,
to die gradually less of disappointment than of scorn. M. Paul
Deschanel had solemnly replaced him. To the most skilful of its
great attorneys, M. Poincaré, the bourgeoisie had entrusted its
portfolios—the war ministry portfolio, which was to all intents and
purposes, the portfolio for reparations. Had not the hour come to
speak to the people in that positive and moralising tone at which it
excels ? " Enough of high-sounding phrases ! In wartime, as at
election time, they are allowed : it is even allowed to exaggerate. But
once the excitement is over, let everyone get on quietly with more
serious activities. We have suffered together, so be it : but you
suffered through your own fault, and we suffered through your
fault, too. Our society was on a very decent basis ; you took
it into your heads to 'want a better one. By unsettling the
established order—the true order, our order—you sinned against
Country, Family, Property, Religion. On this score there is no possible
discussion ; economists, moralists and priests are all agreed. However,

you have now expiated your faults ; let's forget them.   Let us take up
life once more at the point where we left off.   War is not life, no more
than love, poetry and music.   If after the armistice we kept you an
extra year in barracks, it was in order to give you time to clear your
heads of glory and its idle vapours.   In the modern world, the
future is not for heroes but for those who produce goods to
sell, and sell to produce still more goods.   Work, produce, so
that we can sell."
    You in England recognise this sort of talk.   It is exactly what you
hear from Marshal Pétain.   And it is also what the " Rear "—the
famous Rear, the " Hindsides "—once said to us, to us, the men at
the Front, as early as 1919.   The bourgeois élites—political, social,
military, or religious, were already burning in 1919 to summon us to
resignation, expiation, penance.   However confident they may be, or
seem to be, of their own judgment and virtue, they harbour none the
less, in the deepest recess of their conscience, a scruple, a doubt,
perhaps a tinge of remorse.   Why have they built more barricades in
a hundred years than their ancestors in ten centuries ?   I know there
have been pernicious doctrines, duly excoriated in the Encyclicals.
But how did a people so wise, so full of experience and so reasonable
become the gull of uncouth ideologies?   It might have been less through
ill will than through despair.   On certain peculiarly tragic occasions
it is perfectly natural that the bourgeois élites, social, political,
religious or military, should ask the question M. Bovary, the sober and
worthy husband whose wife had just committed suicide, asked over
the body of his charming Emma : " Did I really understand her ? . . ."
And they hope against hope that in the long run the prodigal son will
not only admit he has done wrong, but will take the whole blame on
himself.   " Do not be disturbed : I, and I alone, failed to understand ! "
    God is my witness that I want to speak of these people without
being unjust.   I won't go so far as to say they are making a good thing
for themselves of our calamity, but it is true that they are never more
assured, dignified and eloquent, than in times of national catastrophe.
Convinced that it is nothing to do with them, proud of having foretold
it, they greet catastrophe with the unction of a priest with a grudge
against an elusive parishioner who, when threatened with death,
summons him to his bedside in terror to administer the last sacraments.
I do not accuse them of longing for disaster to come.   But I do insist
that they cannot hate it as I hate it, because for them it represents,
not their punishment, but ours : vindication for all the tedious,
recurrent disappointments inflicted on them by a stiff-necked people
in time of peace.   For the same reason, I insist that they never considered our 1918 victory as more than a stroke of luck we did not
deserve, giving the lie to the prophecies of the wise, Economists,
Moralists, and Business Men . . . At first they did not hate it ; they
accepted it coldly, disdainfully, like the welcome of a solicitor to a
young spendthrift whose ruin he had often foretold, and who brings

him news of an unexpected, unhoped for legacy. What is the good of
that, says the man of law, shrugging his shoulders.

They made us mistrustful of our victory—that is what I cannot
forgive them. They could understand us no better than that. No one
understood us properly. You Americans, for instance, who may read
these pages—I knew your men ; they were fearless boys, much more
foolhardy than ours, but chaps of another genus, another species ;
you will have learnt nothing about us from them. The moral folk
who had been waiting at the Academy of Moral Sciences, forestalling
Marshal Pétain, waiting fifty years for the chance to scold a humiliated,
repentant France, really accused us of having won on a gamble. Indeed
we had done so : won on the gamble of Life and Death, double or
quits. But we had worked hard too, upon my word. We may have
fought without inspiration or genius—but not without patience and
endurance. And if we did not know much about heroism as an art,
we knew it as a trade, we could supply sound craftsmanship, rustic
heroism, built of sound materials, a bit rough and ready, but hard-
wearing.   Why, those fellows greeted us like schoolmasters welcoming
the boys back to school after the holidays. They had left the war to
us ; now they were taking Victory away from us. They looked at it
this way and that, handled it knowingly, pored over it like pawn-
broker's assistants carefully examining the watch we bring them.
Then, wagging their heads, they said with a sigh : " You see, it's not
too good : one can't give you much for that sort of a victory ; but
we'll get the most we can for you."

Of course we should have answered, " Give it back, you fools !
It's only just begun. We grant you that we won it on a gamble—if
that pleases you. That only shows we're having a lucky streak, the
stars are with us ; let's make hay while we can ; forward, march.
Let's play for Peace now, double or quits. Peace for all, forever, a
grand peace, a thundering, God almighty Peace ! " That is what we
should have said. But you were already heroes out of work ; hero or
no hero, a man out of work is only a man out of work. But that is
what our people should have said. However, not on any account
would they have said it. What they could be bold enough to say
they would be bold enough to do, at once, instantly, for they find it
far harder to speak than to act, and to express themselves than give
themselves. The source of their greatness lies not in their imagination
but in their hearts. And those men I'm speaking of were very careful
not to appeal to their hearts. First they silently looked our people
up and down, with that protective air which disconcerts and maddens
them : " Risk the peace ? Get on with you. Why not gamble for
victory while you are about it. Come, come, what childishness. You
know nothing of the value of money, and victory is money. As soon
as you have a hundred francs in your pockets you think you are rich,
you treat the whole world, and there you are, penniless. Put your
victory in the savings bank. We, the social, political and military

élite, are your savings bank, the national savings bank." What could our people answer to that ? They were already looking askance at their victory, wondering whether the diamond was genuine or paste. It was a real diamond, but in the rough. To cut this precious stone, to make it flash forth fire to light the world, would have required all the patience, all the pains, all the heroism which this people had just given to the war. But the men of law locked this precious thing in their safe and the bourgeoisie borrowed on it. The bourgeoisie, not only our own, but yours—in fact the universal bourgeoisie would not stake anything on peace, though the people staked everything on war. Nor have the people forgiven it. Of course it's easy enough to say that the Treaty of Versailles is to blame and that the Treaty of Versailles was badly made. It was badly made—it tried to tackle, as though it were a mere business matter, to be settled by trade methods, the vast adventure on which the world had embarked, almost without knowing it, and which ought to be carried through to the end, at all cost, at any price, in order that mankind should not have hoped in vain. The cost was too great ? Well, war is dearer to-day and when it is over you will find the same problem to solve, the same sacrifices—only heavier.

May, 1941

THE papers tell us that English and French troops are to-day facing one another across the Syrian frontier. It does not matter whether the news is true or false. I know well that it is not within the power of any man to run faster than misfortune. It is not a question of keeping up with it, but of going our own pace, and of moving forward at any cost, because none of our steps is lost. And whatever happens, nothing will be worse than what we have already often seen in the course of history, for it is certainly not the first time our lads face one another, and we must just keep our heads clear. Your nation has never, not even in the days of the Black Prince, stood higher ; never has it been more honourable for men to measure themselves against men. This reasoning may seem a bit odd to your practical sense, but you do not expect me to talk to you like any literary hack. And, to tell you what lies at the back of my mind—having nothing more to lose, we might almost be tempted to welcome this absurd adventure with a sort of bitter joy : the height of absurdity has been attained and to me the most regrettable consequence would be the restoring of some semblance of honour to the generals and admirals of the Defeat, if they were forced to fight. As for the poor irresponsible devils who will stand up to your guns, in the service of Great Germany, I should rather envy them than anything else. Since the armistice, any chance to die is a good one for young Frenchmen.

Though my country's disaster has wounded the quick of my heart, I may testify that it has never seriously troubled my reason, and it is in my reason, not in my heart, that I find the principle of my unconquerable hope. Do not take me for a man of systems and principles. I have no systematic philosophy because such mental processes are a form of insanity ; systems are useful only to fools. Common sense shows us that in their efforts to simplify, they make endless complications, whereas life, while seeming to complicate, simplifies everything. And I have no principles for the simple reason that I feel no need whatever to impose a sort of constitution on my conscience, or to live with my conscience under a constitutional régime. The word *principle*, moreover, has fallen so low through misuse that to describe a man to-day as having principles is almost equivalent to saying that he has a private income. I have no need for principles because I am a Christian ; I have no principles, but a faith ; and that faith, which requires that I love my neighbour, invites me to understand him too, and this is the most sure and loyal way of loving him. And I beg you not to believe, either, that I want to take it out of my contemporaries for not profiting by my teachings. I have deliberately tried to write what I really thought—and when a man deliberately writes what he thinks, he finds he has to put himself through it every day, too, hard though it is, and this rather takes the edge off any pleasure there might be in lecturing other people. Though I actually did foresee some of our misfortunes, I am rather tempted to apologise for it, finding myself among those who, having foreseen them, did not manage to help the world avoid them.

In great dramas like Shakespeare's tragedies—all the great dramas of history are Shakespearean—the same character turns up again and again : with his hands behind him and head thrust forward, he stumbles about among the ruins, repeating endlessly in cavernous tones, " I told them so." Once in a thousand times, he really has the right to say so, and posterity will erect monuments to his name. Nine hundred and ninety-nine times, he is one of life's failures who has always gone about consistently foretelling the worst, and whom the folly of men proves to be right. For a single Chéradame, you will find ten million drivellers whose inspiration is merely liverish. What I have written I have written ; there it is. I should like to write to-day as though I had never written anything. My small testimony is not valuable because of anything to do with me : I am not arguing about my country's disaster, which would be a mean way of detaching myself from it and placing myself above it : I feel it, I suffer it, I am living it and I have lived it for months with all the strength and all the capacity of my life. I invite you to feel it and suffer it with me, because it is yours too ; it is marked with the mark of your sins as well as mine.

Please don't go calling me moralising at this point. It is not a matter of moralising but of understanding. You in England know as well as any of us those silly asses who call themselves politicians because they carry on with idiotic, imperturbable solemnity in the most ludicrous situations, of which any child could see the funny side. No catastrophe catches them unawares. With gravity they turn to the public, gravely they agree that this catastrophe, though terrible to contemplate as imminent, is now occurring in actual fact, and people must trust them, with their sense of reality, to make the best of a bad job; the only evil to fear being their removal from power because, even supposing they did make a mistake, they know that mistake better than anyone else, they have explicit knowledge of it, and consequently they are the most suitable people to remedy it. " History is always making fresh starts ", they say. And they have every intention of making a fresh start themselves. They have lost everything, but they promise to save the rest. The word *save* flatters the blind submission of the sheep as the word *destroy* flatters the blind ferocity of the wolves. Only the wolves destroy what needs saving, and the sheep save what needs destruction : so why bother to distinguish between them ? To save at all costs makes impossible that which might have been ; strangling the future in embryo seems to me no less reprehensible than turning the present topsyturvy, although the former lacks the tell-tale externals of disorder ; and many will certainly agree with me that it is better for a man to be killed than castrated.

If you in England would reflect upon these deep, hidden concordances, you would no longer wonder why world-wide disaster comes gradually to look so gratuitously silly, offuscating your positive minds and your positive sense of life. Events which to you seem weird are much more narrowly linked together than the economists and the law professors would admit. The logic of fools rules their unfolding : that is a fact. I do not at all underestimate the inexorable rigour of such logic, for every fool is in himself but a fool ; but the accumulated experience of fools weighs upon the world with a great weight. The prudence of fools consists in being always wary, for, like certain rudimentary sea-creatures, they can only survive in calm waters ; the least eddy is fatal to them. It is the prudence of fools which modern society, by an amazing abuse of words which would have astonished the ancient Greeks, to-day calls weighing the pros and cons, as though there were any other measure for man than to give himself without measure to values infinitely greater than the field of his own life. But we must not waste our time cursing the fools : they are parasites, and if nature chooses to have parasites, then they are not without their uses. But observation of the animal kingdom unfortunately shows that parasites which are allowed to thrive too long end by imposing their laws of existence upon the superior species at whose expense they live. We do not only support the fools : little by little we conform to the slackened pace of their life ; some day perhaps we shall sacrifice man's creative genius to this will to preserve, in favour of which the promulgators of political doctrine will no doubt produce high-sounding formulæ, but which is in fact the simple reflex action of the fool's instinct for self-preservation.

Will you refuse to believe me when I tell you that my country's disaster is something tremendous, beyond the comprehension of fools ; and that it cannot be made to fit the fool's logical framework ? Is this too much to ask on behalf of an ancient people which has worked so hard, worked for a thousand years ? In the name of his fool's realism, the fool urges you in undertones to cash in on our misfortune. But I say, though it may be in accordance with worldly wisdom, if not with justice, to cash in on errors and mistakes, shame can be exploited only by running the risk of being the partner to it, sooner or later. With the honour of my people, your own is at stake ; it is impossible to build anything whatever upon the dishonour of my country. If you do, you will be making the same mistake as Marshal Pétain, who claims to base his national revolution upon it. To take advantage of our dishonour, you would have to make up to those among us who are responsible for it, and I propose to prove to you now that they belong to a species of men as numerous in England as elsewhere, a species which is scattered throughout the world, whose vocation it is to liquidate, being impotent to create. They are not always dishonest or perverse, but a thousand times more noxious than the dishonest and the perverse when they slyly insinuate themselves into men's consciences to relax their tension ; and having liquidated our honour they will then liquidate yours. The ambition of the dictators could never have expanded in full evil-doing if the hypocrisy of the would-be tactful had not supplied them with a favourable cultural environment, to use a phrase dear to the microbiologists. The term *hypocrisy* may seem to you a bit exaggerated : yet there is no true hypocrisy without an undercurrent of sincerity ; conscious, lucid, coldly-calculating hypocrisy is merely the full-fledged form of duplicity—nothing else—and it does not provoke disgust. What makes the hypocrite an object of disgust, a vile thing, is that lying for him is not a means but an end ; it is because he finds his realisation and fulfillment in the lie, he exists wholly in the lie. He loves it, and there is the secret of his nature. He no longer distinguishes between virtue and its counterfeit ; he reveres his studied, make-believe virtue, and through it he reveres himself ; he almost believes he is sacrificing his life to it, bending every effort as he does to a scrupulous rendering of its exterior ; and he may end by dying in peace, with the hope that such long and persevering effort, so ill-paid by scanty profits in this world, will have its reward in the next. In the end, the hypocrite performs the same services as the honest man ; imitation truth is easier to handle than genuine truth ; it is less dear, men bargain for it. And this last reason is of tremendous importance to the democracies. The democracies, wildly prodigal as regards home concerns, have always administered their foreign propaganda skilfully. What are the bulk of well-known politicians and leaders if not publicity men and loud-speakers aimed at universal public opinion, while the permanent secretaries and government offices get on quietly with the real work ? To play this noisy part, the democracies considered a truly sincere man more dangerous than efficacious : difficult to keep under control. On the other hand an ordinary liar, an out-and-out liar, a cynical and well-disposed demagogue, has too little tact. Hence it was natural that the democracies should secure the co-operation of those double personalities described as moderates, who know how to be moderate—even in their expression of so-called subversive ideas—because they keep at an equal distance from truth and falsehood, and it is impossible to say their intentions are low, as they admit no such thing even to themselves.

It is to such men that for twenty years we entrusted the cause of peace for instance ; they made no demands, they were content to proclaim their desire for peace. What else could they have done ? It was their one wish, they really did mean it ; they really were afraid of war, not only of the perils of war, for most of them were exempt from these on account of age, but of another danger a thousand times more terrible in their eyes, that of losing their jobs and breaking their careers. For they felt deeply incapable of prospering except in peaceful conditions, peace at any price ; they knew that war, or even admitting the risk of war, would promptly strip them of their prestige and return them to the void. In the same way they made as though to serve freedom. They placed their hypocrisy at the service of freedom as at the service of peace ; they did not really love either freedom or peace ; it was what they were used to, and they clung to what they knew as the guarantee of their well-being and comfort. This must not be interpreted too narrowly. I mean also their moral well-being and their spiritual comfort, with their conscience at peace. They preached the Letter, they denied the Spirit ; they sought in the Letter shelter from the Spirit : it is the more or less conscious design of all Pharisees.

In England, you are not, most of you, psychologists, but believe me, it is not for my pleasure that I draw a psychological portrait of the men who were your masters and still claim to be mine ; they fill me with horror, my pen jibs at writing of them. You are not psychologists exactly, but you do know your Bible, you know what a Pharisee is. The Pharisees were not, in any sense, primarily imposters ; they were not just pretending to pray or fast or pay tithes. They conformed to the Law ; they conformed scrupulously, but for one scruple : their hearts did not conform ; and perhaps their hearts were of a different pattern. For months I have thought constantly about my country's calamity, and it seems to me to exceed the scope of a national catastrophe. Do not take this for mere hollow bluster. It is not absurd to see in the yielding of a great people, one of the keystones of the European structure, the sign of a loss of equilibrium throughout.

At the moment, you are too deeply engaged with the enemy ; you will notice the cracks and fissures later on. True enough, we eat frogs, but we have eaten them for a thousand years, and up till now this cold-blooded animal has not lowered our temperature ; one day we may have a feverish attack and set fire to the old house through shame, or remorse, or anger, or simply to see the neighbours' faces. You surely don't suppose that Marshal Pétain, even with the assistance of a general staff of big industrialists, academicians, technicians, cardinals and archbishops, can insure you all against the danger of fire ? The size of the premium would exceed the resources of Europe.

I should now like to call your attention to a fact so important, so obvious, so perfectly clear from the evidence that no one takes any notice of it, like Poe's stolen letter—if you remember. The pace of modern life has increased enormously, which works greatly to the advantage of business men and politicians. But how are the people to keep up with it ? Nations always have moved slowly, thought slowly, spoken their thought slowly, put it into practice more slowly still. And it often happened that their masters beat them in the race ; but the lead was rarely such that they could not eventually catch up, in their heavy-footed way. In the long run it was, after all, the people who made history, their own history, and the politicians were only too glad if they succeeded in leaving some permanent, lucky trace of their passage. Today the business men and the politicians are the makers of history ; the people are always too late—unless some un-expected disaster occurs, an earthquake or landslide barring the way to the nimble exploiters . . . May the mighty hand of God fall upon them !

That is why no one today can predict the coming reaction of my country, nor of yours, nor indeed, of any other country. We have lost touch with the people : that is the bitter truth. Between them and us, circumstances have produced, increased and prospered a sort of middle-men, recruited from all classes, terribly difficult to define, having no particular vices or virtues ; their evil-doing is due to the positions they hold, to which their birth did not entitle them. You will doubtless declare that I am being unjust to the poor devils, with all their good intentions, swollen as they are with good intentions like bladders ; and that I should surely keep my fury for demented, savage, sanguinary men. My answer is that if the people are going mad, it is because the would-be wise are too stupid ; stupidity has made them disgusted with wisdom ; hypocrisy has spoilt their taste for truth. Is it unusual to see sensitive, passionate women, of hitherto excellent lives, go to pieces for having married fools ? But I would prefer to talk about horses, which is a subject you are most familiar with. You know very well that it is enough to mount a young horse—mettlesome, spirited, eager to stretch his legs—with some bragging, chicken-hearted rider, for that horse promptly to turn vicious. My explanation is not without worth ; it is sad that you cannot counter it. For a long time now, a very long time, we have prided ourselves on running the affairs of the world in accordance with the precepts of bourgeois wisdom, bourgeois moderation, and the flattest form of common sense, and all we have done is to provoke a violent attack which has thrown our forecasts to the winds (that goes without saying), and stunned the imagination of the poets. Less than half a century after Queen Victoria's jubilee, the world is hailing the rise of the demi-gods : you cannot find that normal. If someone had foretold that an impoverished little beggar, one of those tramps that you have often seen at nights sleeping in a public square, collarless, the stump of his cigarette still drooping from his lips, was to become the founder of a new religion, you would have burst out laughing. Hitler does not at all look like a demi-god, or even a quarter-god, and we are informed by his cook, doctor and man-servant that he eats, drinks, defecates just like you and me—all that is simple enough. Unhappily the fatal omen is, not the fact (or not) of Hitler being a demi-god, but that he is treated as such, that millions of people should have given themselves over to him, body and soul, expecting to work their redemption. The fatal omen is idolatry, not the idol. And if you reply that idolatry is a well-known, codified phenomenon, I shall point out that circumstances can turn it into quite a new problem ; for in olden times mankind embraced idolatry through ignorance, and today it returns to it through despair. But that is as far as I will go. For the world's despair is indeed the one subject of conversation which your patience and your courtesy cannot long endure.

Jacques Maritain has told you, and I tell you again, that our democracies were diseased. The Weimar democracy as much as M. Nitti's, the democracy of simple-minded Doumergue as much as that of God-fearing Alcala Zamora, dear to the Jesuits ; the democracy of M. Benes, or your own—all the democracies suffered from a kind of disease analogous to the one of which the discovery of vitamins revealed the cause : a deficiency disease ; they were deficient in heroism, pride and honour ; and this disease was deep-seated. You need not trouble to point out that during the last fifty years there has been no lack of heroes. Yes, between 1914 and 1918 we had a double, triple, tenfold supply of heroes ; it reminds one of the man who wanted to swallow in a single gulp some strychnine intended to last him six weeks. And what is the good of heroic actions if their lesson is lost, that is, if heroism is slandered, or, worse still, cunningly undervalued, looked upon as a mere picturesque adjunct to life, a dubious extra, a luxury ? Out of sheer habit, we kept on telling our children the fine tales, but as soon as they were old enough to observe and to reflect, they understood very well that serious folk are realistic. " And they always have been ", you will answer. Maybe. But never before was it stated with such insistence, or shouted so loud from the housetops. Thanks to the immense publicity of the press and the radio, now as never before

it became distinguished to make a dupe of one's neighbour, not merely
as in other days, at a diplomatic conference table, with those in the
know, but in the presence of an innumerable audience. Even the
churchgoers boasted of the Holy See's realistic diplomacy, silly fools
that they were. No sooner was it crowned with success than double-
dealing became legitimate and holy. Never has any prince of this
world, however glorious, just and holy he may have been, received
such unanimous respect, such scrupulous obedience, such abundant
homage, as the new Master of Universal Conformism, His Majesty the
Accomplished Fact. As for the victims, it did not even occur to them
to apologise for being taken in ; like good sports they accepted their
reverses, with a knowing little grin, and anyone who appeared to mind
their attitude would be thought an ill-mannered fellow. This state of
mind is still abroad. Don't we frankly admit now that we made a
mess of the 1918 Peace ? Have we any notion at all what it means to
have messed up a peace which cost five million lives ? And you think
this is just talk ? . . . No, it is not talk ; or else it is talk that carries
terrible destructive power, for by putting such talk down as best he
could in his illiterate jargon, Hitler set Germany on fire.

I apologise for reviving these memories ; I have no other means of
making you understand my country's misfortune—not in order to
crave your indulgence or pity, but to put you on your guard, for it
has still not reached its ultimate conclusions. It is a noxious wound
in Europe's side. So long as heroic blood shall flow, the infection will
perhaps not be virulent, but once you have won the war, it will poison
the peace. I am not one of those who go about moaning and groaning
as though our ghastly adventure were merely a misunderstanding and
a mistake. I say that in the heart of our people there is something
rotten ; although the bacteria which causes this rot may be dissemin-
ated throughout the world, I claim that this focus of infection is the
most dangerous of all and that it must be treated as such. It is not
a matter of sticking on a plaster, imagining that after all, if only
France would keep quiet until the end, the victors will benefit from a
convalescence which will cut her out of the victory. In 1917 you
thought like that about Russia, and it brought you no good luck.
France will not accept shame. Without drawing too much upon
your imagination, you can easily foresee the state of world opinion at
the end of a bloody war. The very men whose mean action to-day
is the turning of France towards dictatorship, will judge us more
harshly than all the rest, and in the name of morals and religion. It
is our bad example which will have perverted pure and spotless consciences, betrayed the good faith and candid piety of the high Italian
clergy, thrust into error upright men like General Franco and General
Antonescu. The moral loneliness of our nation would in such circumstances be one of history's most harrowing tragedies. My country
will not be able to bear it without terrible convulsions. My country

will not bear obloquy ; still less will it bear pity. My country will not rise and find itself after victory ; it must· find itself before. It must save itself while there is still time ; it must be helped to free itself by fire and the sword, instead of gentle treatment meted out to those you so amusingly call the " elements of order ", and who are in fact the corruptors. Certain Catholic journalists in Canada, whom the Spanish crusade caused to lose what little judgement Providence had endowed them with, congratulated themselves last year on Marshal Pétain's armistice having saved France from social disorder. The future holds in store more than one surprise for the fools whose calling it is blindly to sacrifice realities to appearance, conscience to prestige, and the salvation of the flock to the shepherd's wish for a quiet life. Please do not indulge in the folly of hoping that France will wallow in dishonour one day longer than necessary. A dis-honoured France will have no resources for good, but she will retain immense resources for evil.

Believe me, Englishmen, your realists mock you when they claim to judge the importance of events by their political consequences alone. Immediate consequences are deceptive ; and to foresee the long-term consequences of an historical fact, better a thousand times watch its repercussions in the consciences of men. And the depth of those repercussions is measured less by the gravity of the error than by the respectability of the guilty, for it is that which gives scandal. This world's wretchedness lies in the fact that so many indignities have for half a century been worthily committed by worthy men. Worthy men were in other times little known to most poor devils. Like statues of saints and relics, which are carried through the town only on solemn occasions,. the great of the earth kept themselves carefully screened from indiscreet curiosity ; they knew that the old proverb holds—no man is a hero to his valet. To-day, thanks to the newspapers, any small reader may know more about his masters for tuppence than the valet himself, don't you agree ? . . . In consequence, not only can the unworthy acts of worthy men not pass unnoticed, they must also account for them, excuse them and justify them to the public. As in real life comic is never far from tragic, sometimes the drama turns to farce ; the audience never tires of watching all these imposing personages—formerly carved into Cathedral portals—come and go, hand on heart, their eyes popping out of their heads, mopping their brows while they account for themselves like schoolboys caught red-handed. What I say of the great of the earth I could say equally well of the ruling classes, the *élites*. The world has reached a pass where, caught in the spotlight, the microphone always at hand, shot day and night by millions of cameras, the great must elect to be great, the ruling classes, to rule. There will be no getting away with another Munich.

Those who do me the honour of reading what I write know that I am not a pamphleteer. I was sometimes taken for one, when I

violently indicted mediocre men whom everyone considered insignificant. They are so, but the evil they beget is not. Obstinacy, complacency and stupidity are at the heart of all our troubles, and to be
in doubt about this is to have no comprehension of nature, history or
one's own life. But fools only pay attention to what frightens them,
and they are afraid only of violence, whereas violence is almost always
a reaction against stupidity, that is, against injustice. A man of mean
intelligence and heart commits a certain number of acts of injustice
every day, and were each no larger than an ant, what of it ? If you
allow such vermin to multiply they will devastate the world. Ants
frighten no one ; they are none the less the agents of tremendous,
incalculable havoc, as we in this country know only too well. " Either
Brazil will kill the ant, or the ant will kill Brazil " : this remark of a
famous Brazilian has become a national slogan.

France has been the victim of a species of small-minded man all the
more suspect because he seems inoffensive, and kind even. You English
had eyes only for external damage : you saw with dismay disorderly
men flourishing torches around the walls of our old home ; but we had
known for a long time that the inside was a ruin brought about by the
very men you saw mounting guard at the loop-holes, as though they
were defending it, though in fact they were defending only themselves,
that is, their threatened dignity ; perhaps they honestly believed, in
the shadow of imminent bankruptcy, that they ought to save at least
their prestige, cost what it might . . . As I have already said, there is
no lie without its streak of sincerity, and it is by this that one can hope
to know a man ; it is upon this ember still glowing under the ashes
that one must blow to see clearly. Experience has shown me, all too
late, that you cannot explain human beings by their vices, but by
what they have kept intact, unsullied, by the bit of childhood still
left them, however deeply to be sought. You will understand that I
am not referring to M. Laval or to M. Darlan, or any men like them.
These politicians have exploited defeatism as they would have
exploited the spirit of victory ; the whole life of such climbers is a
mere wager, and this time the wager was on cowardice : that is all.
But one fact must have struck you. Some found it possible to believe
that our military failure brought about another one—the rout of our
consciences. If the spirit of failure had beset all consciences, the first
to give way would have been the ones with fewest defences, the lowest
and meanest. This is not how it was. The armistice was not the
despairing gesture of a panic-stricken parliamentarian, but a considered action, carried out in cold blood with the kindly but inexorable
authority of a bailiff seizing a bankrupt's goods or a surgeon opening
a painful abscess. No one should say that this Marshal, so oddly
become the impassive executor of the judgments of the Enemy, was
trying to give decent utterance to the blind renunciation of a fear-
maddened mob : this is an even greater error. Neither Marshal
Pétain nor anyone else could at one fell stroke have handed over Paris,

the fleet and the Empire without the support of a substantial body of public opinion, and this body of opinion was perfectly aware of its responsibility. There was, there always has been, an armistice party, favouring renunciation and defeatism, and this party was not recruited among the ignorant masses of the people—you know this as well as I do by now, I hope. If the word *élite* still has any meaning, that party was recruited among the élites ; it is even the élite of the élite . . . Am I exaggerating ? Certainly not. It would have been reasonable to think, for instance, that since certain democratic measures had considerably increased the number of officers risen from the ranks, men with the reputation of behaving more like small needy bureaucrats than soldiers, they would be the first to support a policy so obviously inglorious. Not at all : it was the well-educated, cultured army officers, the aristocratic " right-thinking " elements in the Navy, that spoke out spontaneously, passionately, furiously, in favour of peace at any price.

This is not an indictment of the élites as such. Demagogues have a grudge against the governing classes because they govern ; I have a grudge against them because they do not govern enough, because they have lost their sense of the responsibilities of leadership. How absurd it is to see the very men who for ten years have prided themselves on representing and incarnating the principal of authority—the leaders of industry, the military, aristocracy, churchmen—proclaiming the necessity of dictatorship, and thus proclaiming their own impotence. Such a thing has never been seen before. Throughout the whole course of history, dictatorship has always been a crude and powerful instrument for the use of the masses, the only means they had of brutally imposing their will, unable as they themselves were to express or even clearly to conceive it. " We give you our power ", they said to the dictator. " We deposit in you our passions and our hopes ; you are to be our brain ! " This is why a dictatorship of the proletariat may be a regrettable phenomenon ; it none the less accords with the nature of things. Surely you would not have wished the Russian mujiks to have formed an aristocratic Republic or a corporative Monarchy on the rotten remnants of czarist bureaucracy, régimes of such complexity being scarcely within the powers of poor wretches suddenly set free of their masters, but not alas ! free of the habits and vices of long-term serfdom. That any élite should enthusiastically support such primitive modes of government, when the one justification for its existence is the achievement of a higher form of political organisation : that is enough to cloud our minds, did we not know the answer to the riddle ; what these degenerate élites expect of dictatorship is for it to take over the power with its risks, leaving them the prestige and the profit.

The tragedy of my people is a tragedy of conscience ; the conscience of my people has yielded. I do not deny that the blame rests on us

all ; but it is certainly legitimate to place the primary responsibility
on those who, because of their status, education and calling, were
supposed by all and sundry to be the highest form of that national
conscience.   It would be all too easy and mean to make poor devils,
half aware or totally unaware of the issue, responsible for a crisis of
conscience ! I am not trying to make you see this crisis as I see it ;
I only want you to endeavour to judge it according to your own lights,
instead of falling back, as you have done hitherto, on the judgement
of literary mountebanks and parlour prophets whom you foolishly
mistake for thinkers because they write books, or even for men of the
world because they used to take tea at the Ritz . . . They naturally
give you what you want : it is their job and their function to please
their customers ; so they produce reassuring conclusions, and turn
France's disaster into a topic like any other, a scandal in politics
and high society in which they are proud to play a part.   I do beg
you to leave these idiots to the smoking room, lavatory, nursery—
anywhere ; and let us speak as men to men.   Is it normal that an old
nation, the crown of Europe, should suddenly be seen not only in
total military collapse, but—what is a thousand times more astonishing
—in a fit of wilful, collective self-abasement at the feet of a conquerer :
this is without precedent in all our history, or even our literature,
excepting perhaps the " Confessions " of Jean-Jacques Rousseau ;
and is more reminiscent of the wild and dreary conceptions of the
Russian novel.   No nation, not yours nor mine, can declare itself
immune from despair.   Suppose it comes to that.   The nation in
despair remains itself, even so ; it despairs in its own way, and however
anguish may disfigure it, no one who has loved it will for a moment
fail to recognise the familiar tone of voice, the well-loved features.
But why talk of *despair ?* If my nation despaired to-day, it would
despair as it never has despaired ; its despair would bring us all more
bitter deception even than its collapse.   But it does not in fact seem
to be despairing at all ; no more does it appear to have any hope.   It
is just enduring, and in its acquiescence in the accomplished fact, its
punishment and imposed expiation, it seems to find some horrible
sort of relief.   It does not show regret for having once been great, but
only at having believed it was ; it has made itself at home with its
humiliation and is getting on with life on those terms busily, almost
cheerfully, as though the famous " safety first " policy, with which
for twenty years it wearied the world, were at long last revealing its
inner meaning and reaching fulfillment—safety in withdrawal and
oblivion.

You may point out that nations are no less subject than individuals
to breakdowns of personality, suddenly laying bare the shameful
elements in their souls.   But you know our people, and I do too.
Extreme misery has often turned it brutal and cynical, sometimes
cruel.   Never has it been seen looking so respectable in servitude,
with its would-be worthy bearing and its smug expression, as though

it had been caught in a house of ill-fame and was declaring its intentions to be of the best, the scheme being, under divine guidance, to win back to virtue, religion and piety the proprietor of the establishment, his wife, his girls and their pimps. My country loathes Tartuffe ; or rather, it is saved from him by something better than loathing : it it has never done him the honour of taking him seriously. Hypocrisy doesn't work with our people because it makes them laugh. The final contradiction would be for them to become ridiculous to themselves, themselves turning sanctimonious and bigoted.

These home-truths may be painful to many in England. Those who are now betraying you belong to the same breed you humoured in Italy, and which you insist on still humouring in Spain ; you even humour them in your own country. Habits of speech bind men together, and the turn of phrase used by these fellows resembles your own. They betray you, if I may put it so, in the very terms they would have used to defend you, if it had been in their interest to defend you. Does their policy really remind you of nothing ? How very odd. It strikes me as very like the non-intervention business in Spain. And our famous New Order—don't you recognise it either ? Yet we set it going together. But in those days it was M. Benes who served as propitiatory victim, and if you were not actually holding the sacrificial knife, you were wearing, as we were, the white robes of the neophite and you had your share of the purifying blood. Do you really find it odd of me to compare weak men to violent men ? But everyone knows that violence is only an aspect of weakness. Whenever a man proclaims that power sets him above honour, it is a safe bet that weakness will set him beneath it ; weakness or power will supply him with exactly the same pretext for forswearing his obligations. Nothing is more absurd than the wry faces and contortions of so many Catholics to-day in their efforts to escape these truths. They must allow me to add that the very weakness of the Vichy Government's attitude to the conqueror is the clue to the violence and rage in repression it would display, were foreign support to enable it to emerge victorious from a civil war.

In spite of all this, you will doubtless continue to lay the blame for your faults and ours on the poor devils ; you will say once more that the masses have become ungovernable, without ever once troubling to enquire whether the élites have not become incapable of governing. I could not possibly share your point of view; it makes me feel physically sick, and all well-born Frenchmen feel the same, I hope. You are a race of daring fellows, whereas we are less adventurers than soldiers ; we are a military race : we know by instinct that it is dishonourable for an officer to blame his short-comings on those under his command. If this is not reason sufficient, let me add that I am a Christian. As a Christian, no shame can fall on me directly, not even from the Holy Father, because I know myself and I know what is in man ; but the thought of scandal given to the little ones is unbearable.

After all, why should you not agree with me ? Will you still reproach the French people for their previous lack of faith in military, ecclesiastical and worldly dignitaries who have since, of their own accord, put their services at the disposal of the enemy ?

The crisis of June, 1940, might have been, like 1918, one of sheer physical and nervous exhaustion, the final crisis in a long process of weakening. But we were beaten, not exhausted. It might also have been a gesture of despair : the champion giving up, Marshal Pétain throwing up the sponge. The latter explanation pleased you immediately through its simplicity. All you had to do was to show the boxer, the victim of a moment's weakness, a sportsmanlike forbearance. But a strange thing happened ! The aged manager received your cordial message with extreme coldness. You probably felt that a gentleman always finds it a little embarrassing to say thank you ; you never suspected that he was engaged in counting the cash, with the secret intention of putting it all in his own pocket.

After all, it would have been much more satisfactory for you if you had, then and there, gone straight to the boxer, to the French people themselves, and shown up the crafty scheming of the management. M. Laval's bid for power, carefully prepared in Rome and Madrid, had little chance of success without the support of the Marshal ; the Marshal was indispensable to M. Laval as surety, and you were careful not to question its worth. It was the Marshal who gave surety for M. Laval, and you put up the bond for the Marshal, who in turn gave bail for Hitler. Your esteem was excessive beyond all measure. Hearing you talk about the Victor of Verdun, one might have believed that the armistice was signed not only by this military man, but by the three hundred and fifty thousand dead in the Douaumont charnel-house. " Well," said the French, " we had been inclined to think that we hadn't played fair. But since the losers themselves implore us to look upon the Marshal as incarnating all the civil and military virtues, we should be silly to have any doubts. So distinguished an old gentleman obviously cannot have incited us to play an underhand game."

So you in England made things easy for the Marshal ; and still more, through the Marshal, for the so-called honest men, the good honest folk, the worthy people, " hombres dignos." For, in contrast to M. Laval or M. Darlan, who represent nothing at all but themselves, Marshal Pétain admirably represents the class from which you expect salvation to come because, as it calls itself the middle-class, it may seem to you probably the most accessible to middling arguments, and less difficult and costly to win over. What a mistake ! It is both credulous and distrustful, sceptical and unimaginative, as any broker or insurance agent used to its way of doing business could have told you. I quite understand your thinking that by keeping on the right side of these excellent folk—each one of whom, taken singly, is an honest man, incapable of signing an unsupported cheque and punctual in the payment of his dues—you would in due course win from them the admission that it is a dirty trick to break a contract with the frank intention of cashing in on the occasion. But this is an even more serious mistake than the other. You forget that as regards everything which is not explicitly defined in the Civil Code, and approved or condemned by the Civil Code, these men claim to be guided by their conscience alone, and you appraise that conscience now too generously, now too harshly. Their conscience may be able to keep them clear of disgraceful acts, but once one has occurred, conscience will not make them admit it, for to do so would be to strike at their prestige, which is one with the prestige of Order, Morality, Religion. A great many of them have been brought up as Catholics ; the Clergy instructed them in all good faith. Unhappily it is not their lessons they remember ; most of them remain indifferent parishioners ; it is the type of mind of the clergy which affected them : what clergyman, of whatever church, ever admitted he was in the wrong ?

You in England have let the time slip by when it was still possible to shame these weak souls : you have allowed them time to construct their own moral code, and now they are firmly entrenched, and you cannot move them. There is a code for the armistice, a code for collaboration, and to-morrow there will be a code for an economic and military alliance, which like all the rest will be granted the benevolent sanction of the spiritual authorities. All these people are in perfect accord with their conscience, and that is what you will not heed. They have set out on a new way of life ; they have not even kept any bad feeling where you are concerned : they would be delighted to exchange greetings, if they met you in the street, for they are sticklers for convention. I will not go so far as to say that they like you, but they will gladly forgive the harm they have done you, if you agree to say no more about it ; what most annoys them is the way you disturb their work and prevent them from getting on with it, for the liquidation of a bankruptcy is a difficult job, a task for expert accountants and actuaries ; so when you come with your palaver about honour, they are cross at having their counting put out for such trifles. Far from making them feel uncomfortable, you confirm their high opinion of themselves ; you give them a sense of secret hilarity, like the old lawyer listening to the awkward assurances of a nephew in need of cash. They pride themselves on being far more honest than you, and they are honest in their way : they would sell France with not a penny out, and with an inventory in perfect order ; if they had their way, everything would be scrapped : not even for remembrance' sake would they retain a scrap of the banner of Austerlitz or the bone of a dead hero—nothing. They have no honour, but they have a conscience ; such a case is far less rare than people think. They have no honour : perhaps they would frankly admit the fact ; they certainly do not feel ashamed of it. It may be taken for granted that they have carefully entered on their ledgers all that honour, the prejudice of honour, and the vain scruples of honour, have cost France during the last thousand years ; and that they could tell you to the last jot and tittle what this wastage represents in calves, cows, sheep, donkeys, game, highways and works of art—in a word, useful expenditure. They have no honour, but they have a conscience. I wrote in another letter about how you English live on too ceremonious terms with your conscience : the household they set up with theirs is more like an old bachelor married to his cook. They have a conscience, but far from expecting to learn from it, they intend to lose no opportunity of giving it some lessons themselves ; they would never put up with a conscience that was lacking in respect and behaving like an emancipated, revolutionary sort of conscience, speaking out without waiting to be asked. In return they require only domestic duties, keeping drawers tidy and polishing the floors.

Such fellows are not monsters at all : their breed is well known to all of us ; we number among them relatives and friends. They have their characteristic qualities and virtues. They are even capable of certain sacrifices, provided they are not too big. How can we call it a crime if, having been born to save, hoard and preserve, this breed preserves, hoards and saves itself, at the expense of a world which it must know it cannot reform. It is not my business to condemn these people ; I merely seek to carry on my unpretentious job as observer of society, and reckon their responsibilities in the catastrophe which threatens the existence of my country. I do not claim that the world will be saved by the masses or the instinct of the masses, " the movements of the masses ", as the petty bourgeois intellectuals of Communism put it in their peculiar jargon. The world will be saved by élites. My country's disaster proved that new élites are needed, or, better, seeing we have some already, a new spirit in the élites ; and they must find their souls again. Had I written these words two years ago, you could have laughed at me. But you would likewise have laughed had I told you at that time what I thought of our ambassador in Madrid, Marshal Pétain. Perhaps the clear-sighted few would have granted that the conscience of our élites was a bit wobbly, but never that it was warped. Was it, or was it not ?

At the time I was talking of the French élites and their excitement over the Spanish " crusade ", a noble example which they burned to follow, I respectfully expressed my doubts, not on the brilliance and polish of their conscience, but on the quality of its metal, well-tempered or no ; and I was sardonically invited to compare it to the working-class conscience. It was a mere quibble. Had the workers' conscience been of even cruder stuff, still the danger would have seemed to me much less great. All the parts of a machine are not made of the same steel. The conscience of the élites is needed for both precision and resistance : the material must be perfect. Yet it did not stand up under sudden stress. It would have been better if it had broken to pieces. Unhappily it was only bent. The motor continues to run, and at each explosion a connecting rod rattles in the crank-case.

We know very well that it takes only a little carbon more or less to change the molecular cohesion of high quality steel. The conscience of our élites lacked an indispensable element, or at least was short of it. It lacked a sense of honour. This is an old deficiency. Our élite is bourgeois, and the bourgeoisie has always mistrusted honour. The absolute nature of honour offends its taste for moderation and measure in all things. In this it is at one with the pious, who see it as a snare for pride. Moreover, the very name recalls old humiliations which still sting, and days gone by when trade was considered derogatory; it sounds in its ears as does the word *noble*, once a source of hatred and envy. Honour, in short, was naturally prodigal, and the bourgeoisie has avarice in its entrails; it remains miserly in the most extravagant luxury; it is sometimes spendthrift out of vanity or insolence, or even virtue; but never liberal and magnanimous by choice or vocation or for pleasure.

I am not here to teach you Englishmen the history of France; I should find it humiliating to take up the defence of my country's past. I do not claim that it was always above reproach. Heaven forfend! But it is full to overflowing with honour. The men of my country have loved honour to the point of ridicule and absurdity: if I may say so, they would have suffered dishonour for honour's sake. Nor do I pretend that they despise money and throw it away as freely as Poles or Russians. But the moment a Frenchman had achieved independence, he would have been ashamed to be taken for one of those for whom we reserve the most insulting words in the language a skinflint (fesse-mathieu), a tightwad (grigou) a niggard (chiche), a sordid fellow (crasseux) a close-fisted chap (lésineur), a haggler (liardeur), a greedy fellow (rapiat), a miser (pingre), a pinch-penny (ladre). In your country, avarice was a mere gentleman's foible. In France it has always been a low-down vice. The novelists of the nineteenth century have made the tight-fistedness of our peasants notorious. This vice is of much more recent origin than is commonly supposed. Earlier writers have left us their picture of the peasant as a good, simple-minded yet astute fellow, cautious in town, authoritative in the village and home, sober by sheer necessity, a heavy eater and drinker when occasion offered, interested in everything and hospitable. J.-J. Rousseau, on the eve of the Revolution, saw him thus. But he was possibly more sorely tried by the development of capital and industry than anyone else, for though the speculative whirlwind passed him by, he had, nonetheless, to witness the degrading spectacle and suffer its revolting contact. He became miserly step by step as he ceased to be Christian. There is the striking double process. The peasant of old France was naturally careful of his time, his land, his stock, but so far from miserly that it has taken the dealers over a

century to scatter abroad the household treasures that had accumulated
in the villages, the simple and magnificent pottery, the furniture
carved in the living wood, and even those embroideries and laces,
kerchiefs and coifs which elegant women of the bourgeoisie were still
haggling over, paying enormous prices, until quite recently.   Old
France had generosity and honour in its very marrow.   It was a
Christendom of the heroic kind. A peasant and military Christendom :
that is what you must understand.   And you must also understand
how immensely difficult, under such circumstances, was the advent of
the bourgeoisie, and the establishment of the bourgeois state and
dictatorship of money.   Despite all the transgressions of the monarchy
since Louis XIV, which opened the way, the process was impossible
without a bloody revolution—one subsidised by foreigners and paid
for by you English—the collapse of our finances and our national
currency, the despoiling of a million legitimate property-owners
through exile or the scaffold, an almost complete reversal of religious,
moral and social values, and the destruction or at least the systematic
disparaging of the old way of life, right down to its simplest traditional
customs.   The advent of the bourgeoisie cost us all that, and still it
would have failed in its undertaking, had not the iron hand of Napoleon
erected for it that political, juridical and administrative framework
within which it has survived.

These historical considerations are very much to the point.   As long
as politicians and diplomats remain indifferent to the psychology of
nations, and judge the psychology of nations by that of their transitory
rulers, or by the result of the last elections, they will be the gulls of
adventurers like Hitler, who have at least a crude, intuitive sense of
this psychology, if no clear and lucid knowledge of it.   Hitler had
precisely the same notion as I had of the profound cleavage, daily
growing more acute, between our people and its élites.   His stroke of
genius was to bring to bear the whole weight of his labour of corruption, not on the masses, which are supposed to be easier to fool,
but upon the élites.   He attacked the supposedly most reliable consciences, and those he had no hope of corrupting he undermined and
set at sixes and sevens with themselves, puzzling over half truths in
opposition and multiplying incompatibilities, all by means of a truly
devilish casuistry.   It may happen to any man, or any nation, to find
itself seriously threatened in its moral unity when face to face with seemingly contradictory duties, and saints and heroes are not exempt from
such trials.   Nothing can be done by discussion : such an experience
demands of a man the risk and surrender of his whole being.   It is
honour which takes such risks ; honour which reacts for us.   Hitler
knew that our élites would offer only scruples.   If Jeanne d'Arc had had
no more than scruples to support her against the judges of the Rouen
Tribunal, those expert theologians would easily have succeeded in
overcoming them.   She stood on her oath.   The devil himself, the
most skilful of theologians and casuists, is powerless against an oath.

Hitler knew that our élites were incapable of this elementary reaction of honour, and that they would examine the risks with the idea of resigning themselves to the lesser ; whereas the least risk was to perish with honour. So the merits and virtues which the Vichy men affect are of no account ; nor is the possible sincerity of their good intentions. Were they to assume monks' habits and sing Pater nosters night and day, I would still take them for sham monks, and the prelates who bless them I would consider legitimate heirs of the Bishop of Beauvais. " If you abjure, you are damned'! " Jeanne d'Arc's saints spoke to her without mincing their words, and if she had indeed persisted in abjuring, retracting, submitting ; if she had spent the rest of her life in a convent, fasting on bread and water, what would she have been but a failure in heroism and Sanctity, the worst kind of failure.

When I write this sort of thing, I care less than nothing for the approbation of politicians. A politician who is merely a politician always seems to me unimportant, but nowadays he is just a fool. His ingenious recipes are as useless, in the present state of the world, as those of an insurance agent who tries to sell his services to an unhappy wretch watching his house burn down and seeing his wife and children in the heart of the furnace ; I care less than nothing for the approbation of politicians. But when Hitler is a prisoner in some dungeon, should he happen to read these lines for lack of better distraction, he will doubtless think I understood him far better than Mr. Chamberlain did. Hitler feared above all the reaction of national honour, and he knew it was not to be expected immediately from the mass of the French people. The masses react slowly. Our people is quite capable of choosing the way of honour, and it can be relied upon to choose it; but it must be shown the way, or it will find it only after much wandering. Then for a century or two our people had no longer lived in the climate of honour.

You English are a nation of seafarers and traders. We are a people of peasants ; we are, to use Péguy's term, a military peasantry ; this fact has tremendous importance. What I was saying just now about our peasants I could have said about all of us. The coming of the Capitalist Order and the dictatorship of economics hit us hard. The economists, who don't know much, know at least that the sudden prodigious rise of your industry towards the end of the eighteenth century was the principal cause of the financial difficulties of our monarchy, difficulties which its experts could not solve because they had never met them before. The old Bourgeois Order sprang from bankruptcy just as Marshal Pétain's new bourgeois order sprang from defeat. It was the worthlessness of the assignat which made possible the vast speculation in landed property and the mass expropriation of ecclesiastical and aristocratic holdings, confirmed by Napoleon's legislation. This legislation made the bourgeoisie master of the State, by furnishing it with the indispensable social prestige

and the money resources necessary for its future speculations. The
bourgeoisie had seized power ; now it had only to exercise it. It is
no exaggeration to say that it found itself in the position of the parvenu
who, having acquired an historic estate, wonders how to get himself
respected and honoured as the former masters were. No, no, it looks
easy enough to-day, but it was no simple matter to impose on our
people the Money hierarchy ! No, no, it was not so simple to bend the
proudest and most independent people in the world, who had known
only the vagabond and happy go-lucky forms of poverty, to the
common misery : the organised, disciplined misery of the mine and
factory ! The bourgeoisie held the reins, of course, but, thank God, in
those days a French bourgeois was neither a fascist nor a nazi. The
idea of legitimacy was so deeply ingrained in the spirit of old France
that this parvenu, like Napoleon himself—had no other idea but to
become himself legitimate. He hoped not only to be obeyed but to
be respected, honoured, and, if possible at not too great a cost to himself, to be loved. He never was so foolish as to undertake to create a
moral system as Hitler did ; he did at least try, by his own cunning,
to adapt the old system to his needs, his tastes and beliefs. So in a
land where the nobility enjoyed so high a status that their title deeds
were their only warrant, he made of Property a sacred right, a Divine
Right, whereas Christianity had declared it to be simply a responsibility
or a duty. Basing his power on the almost absolute control of Labour
by Capital, he made Work into a Religion. Whereas our excellent
forebears simply looked upon work as a penitential obligation, an
expiation of original sin. The Bourgeois laid it piously on altars, next
to Property. " Work is prayer ", was his sententious answer to the
miner or weaver who timidly claimed the right to rest on the Sabbath.
Finally, anxious to keep wages as low as possible, but at the same time
to salve his conscience by offering the workmen a chance to grow rich
without any threat to his own profits, he made Savings the third person
of his Holy Trinity : Property, Work, Savings.

You must admit that such an ideal would unavoidably appear a
little threadbare to a people which, as early as the twelfth century,
described itself in these terms in an immortal prayer which I beg you
to allow me to quote : *O God, who established the empire of the Franks
to be the instrument of Your Divine Will throughout the whole world,
the Standard-bearer of your Glory and the Rampart of Your Holy Church,
we entreat You that Your celestial light may always and in all places so
light and quicken the sons of France turned towards You, that, seeing
what should be done to establish Your Kingdom on this earth, they may
have the courage to accomplish it with tireless energy and charity. Amen.*
The French of the nineteenth century did not seem, at first glance, to
be particularly concerned with the Kingdom of God ; they had in
fact given it another name : they called it Liberty, Equality, Fraternity.
It was inscribed on their standards ; and one cannot for a moment
suppose that the volunteers of *l'An Deux* would have set out to march

across Europe to the sound of the Marseillaise, in the name of Property, Work and Savings ! I showed you one aspect of the Revolution just now ; perhaps I should say, one aspect of the exploitation of revolutionary idealism. To see it merely as an explosion of anti-social and anti-religious fanaticism is to do a great injustice to our people. For, after all, it was the Encyclopædist bourgeois intellectuals, almost all of them educated by the Reverend Jesuit Fathers, who unleashed against Christianity the campaign of slander which cleared the way for the expropriation of Church property. They objected only to Church property and to the teaching of the Gospels, which they found, as Hitler did, much too idealistic, utterly remote from their practical and positive attitude to life. But this point of view had little chance of winning over the French people. Seeing it was impossible to turn public opinion both against the Gospel and against the priesthood, a pretence was made of exalting the Gospel the better to overcome its ministers, convicted of betraying its spirit. Unfortunately, as soon as the people had taken in that priests were merely imposters, they gladly watched them go to the guillotine, just as, five hundred years earlier, they would have watched the burning of witches or of heretics. As long as the legal formalities of expropriation continued, the bourgeoisie naturally could not give free expression to its humanitarian feelings, but once the formalities were over, the execution began of the former executioners, who had expected rather the rewards of civic virtue for having so well avenged the sans-culotte Christ upon his charlatan representatives.

May I be forgiven for speaking in such terms of so tragic a misunderstanding, and for insisting on its clownish aspect. It has continued up to our day, though in different forms. One could give this alternately comic and bloody farce a title : " Journey through History of a Realistic Bourgeoisie and an Idealistic Nation." The realistic bourgeoisie did not have to wait for Mussolini to believe in its realism. It believes in it, loves it and has always been distressed at seeing so many people unmoved by the Cartesian evidences. It has seized every chance to show off its realism : but the French people gave it so chilly a welcome that the bourgeoisie had to put its god back in the strong box quickly and invent a new idealism on the spot. For lack of adepts to its cold, technical and polytechnical mysteries, it had to endure in silence the astounding transformations which the French people wrought upon its most cherished notions ; thus it found itself committed to a series of impostures—the Napoleonic imposture, the democratic imposture and the imposture of Progress. It was, for instance, the Napoleon of the Civil Code whose prestige and favour it wished to secure, but it was to the Napoleon of legend that the hearts of the French people went out, and willy-nilly, for twenty years, the bourgeoisie had to remain captive of a military epic, and to observe the ceremonies of a new cult which it disclaimed at heart. This dangerous fever for glory once lulled, the government of Louis Philippe

seemed to provide the perfect setting for a safe and comfortable
ideology, reasonable too : the bland realisation of the famous slogan :
Property, Work, Savings.   It saw democracy as a policy.   But our
incorrigible people immediately turned it into a faith, a risk, even a
universal risk.   Horrified by this new surge of passion, the bourgeoisie
had no better luck with the myth of Progress, borrowed from the
intellectuals and guaranteed by Science.   When it said " Progress " it
meant the development of Industry and the spread of machinery,
comfort and luxury.   But the people had no use for machinery, comfort
or luxury.   They immediately seized upon this pale nursling of the
laboratories and filled him with their strong wine, and within their
sturdy arms he became all at once the redeemer of the world, the
liberator of the peoples, the Prince of Peace . . . And at each fresh
experience, the dumbfounded bourgeoisie could but regret the days
when these extravagantly imaginative fellows, instead of falling
passionately for abstractions, simply worshipped God.

I apologise for thus making the bourgeoisie perform and hold forth
like an actor on the stage.   I know that a social class is a very complex
organism, and the one with which I am concerned is, in principle,
open to all, and has taken on a new lease of life many times in the last
hundred and fifty years.   It is its attitude which has not budged.
The bourgeois conception of life is no challenge to the imagination,
but on the other hand it gives little scope for contradiction ; it is
thickset, short and stolid.   What alternative could the few thousand
men of the people offer, who in each generation cross the threshold of
the sanctuary ?   They quickly become bourgeois, and even more
bourgeois than the rest.   (This is not the case with Marshal Pétain,
who comes from the humblest of the humble.)   I want you to realise
that, far from having doubts about itself, the bourgeoisie has streng-
thened its conviction that it is the very essence of order, decency,
dignity, logic, and two-and-two-make-four.   What is your answer to
people who claim to be permanently at the point of equilibrium of
forces, the happy mean ?   " Neither reaction nor revolution " seems
to me the most typical of irrefutable axioms ; made up as it is of two
negatives, two refusals, it closes all discussion before it could begin.
Far from giving it qualms, disappointment and mishap have brought
the bourgeoisie precisely what it waited for so long, without daring to
say so : the indisputable and (let us say) religious consciousness of its
legitimacy.   As long as the bourgeoisie was wealthy and in control,
it might still secretly be ashamed of its origins.   Born of bankruptcy,
beneficiary of a colossal expropriation, it had indeed become, almost
at once, the guardian and symbol of Property.   But the Army remained
suspicious for a long time, seeing it as the hostile civil power ; and so
did the clergy, whose influence and prestige it envied while seeming to
disdain.   And now the progress of Socialism forced it to have done
with compromise, for it could not come to terms on the principle of
property without giving way altogether.   Supported by the army and

blessed by the clergy, it felt itself for the first time the real moral and spiritual heir of those it had once despoiled.

Of course this did not happen overnight. We may be sure that its endless misunderstandings with the people had deeply and greatly embittered it against them. But this it did not admit. The word *reactionary* made it feel ashamed, and dishonoured it, it considered, in the eyes of the intellectuals. And when the intellectuals began to rehabilitate both the word and the thing, their efforts threw it into utter bewilderment. Thus, it had taken the Maurras doctrine for no more than paradoxical pub talk, a crazy invention of the *provençal* imagination. Not that it disliked the ideas of this frail little man, so sagacious and so perverse, one of the most dangerous men of our history, but it turned to him only in private, not wanting to be caught. And then, Mussolini . . .

July, 1941

YOU English must get your facts right, and try to understand. Your economists and your politicians would account for class struggles statistically ; I tell you that a class consists of loving, suffering, dying men, and that though conflicts between classes, as between nations, may for a long time be purely economic phenomena, sooner or later they turn into dramas of passion. My country's drama was a family affair ; its tragedy is far more homely than people think. I know very well that speaking as I am about to do, I shall run head on into certain of your prejudices, for you learnt your history at school. You have your history provided by professional historians devoid of any sense of humour, and in no way qualified to settle questions they themselves scornfully dub sentimental. What I have said about our people can be summed up in a phrase. Throughout the nineteenth century and up to the time when it believed, alas ! that it had found a new Christendom in the workers' International, with Stalin as its new Pope, France was a lost child. You are free to think what you will of the old French social order ; you will not refuse to agree that for a thousand years the people of France was able to make itself at home and to build up its customs within its framework. Everything they touched had been used by the forefathers. Don't think that they left home of their own accord. Even the schoolteachers will tell you that in 1789 our people had no intention of moving out ; it was the bourgeoisie which dispossessed them—that's all—promising them a new home in the Bourgeois Commonwealth, where, however, the people have not felt at home at all. And this structure was much newer than you may realise. Lenin was perfectly right when he remarked that our French Revolution, though out of date now, still remains the prototype of all revolutions, because it was, all things considered, much more radical than the Bolshevik revolution, and a

greater shock to the consciences of men. Once the old home had gone,
France was a lost child, a foundling : graciously taken in by bourgeois
society.   No doubt in earlier times it would have found refuge in the
Church.   But the Church itself had lost prestige and wherewithal in
the holocaust.   The Church had to come to terms with the Bourgeoisie ;
it was from the budget of the bourgeois State that the Church now
drew its income ; it was powerless but to prompt the poor orphan to
obey its new masters.   Remember that our whole workers' organisation,
the fruit of so many centuries of toil, had been swept away with the
rest ; our people were stripped of status and proofs of identity ; they
had been turned into tramps and vagabonds.   " Think yourself lucky
that I don't turn you over to the police", said the bourgeoisie.   " I
provide board and lodging.   Now get to work ! "   I do not intend
to-day to discover how our people were boarded and lodged ; but I
want once more to call your attention to the misunderstanding which
has gone on working itself out ever since, now tragic, now laughable,
with pitiless lôgic.   For a hundred years the bourgeoisie obviously
never understood what sort of vagabond it had taken in hand.   As he
had no shirt to his back, it treated him like a savage, a primitive
tribesman.   Recognising no social value but education and money,
and wilfully and desperately ignorant of the qualities of breeding, it
undertook to educate him according to bourgeois methods and the
bourgeois moral code.

I have already referred to a contemporary history of my country
which might be entitled " Adventures and Misadventures of a Realistic
Bourgeoisie and of an Idealistic Nation."   One could also call it :
" Discomfiture of a Petty Bourgeoisie Who, without Knowing it,
Had Harboured the Son of a Great Prince, Formerly Kidnapped by
the Gipsies."   It is useless for you to tell me that the tutor had the
same blood in his veins as his mysterious pupil.   Of course.   But the
people remained natural, or, as we put it in our Paris slang, " nature."
They almost always act spontaneously, according to instinct, which
means, according to hereditary reflexes.   Whereas the bourgeoisie
made itself—" I am a self-made man ", proudly proclaims the bourgeois
parvenu.   It made its own conscience, morality, and spirit.   Its
conception of life gradually became much more social than human, and
it is precisely their human quality that gives the people their worth.
Like all aristocrats, they are born individualists.   The bourgeoisie
takes them for anarchists.   It is exactly the same mistake it made
about Lyautey and Clémenceau, and would make to-day about any
man of old France, for those men were not moderates, as it prefers
them to be.   I despair of making myself understood except by a few,
either in this hemisphere or the other, but you English at least know
what a well-bred people is.   The expression *well-bred* naturally does
not belong to the vocabulary of the bourgeoisie, and in substituting
the expression *well-brought up*, the bourgeoisie believes that it is using
a synonym.   Or it pretends to believe it.   I used to wonder how, so

seemingly proud of its social superiority, it had nonetheless come to adopt towards the people an attitude less of disdain than of surly anger, which resembles a surreptitious kind of envy. The truth is that it cannot forgive the people for making it mistrust itself, its principles and its wisdom. This crude, foul-mouthed foster-child, so obviously not fitting in with the ideal of the substantial citizen and " big-wig ", from which it expected, as of right, the humble and fervent admiration of Man Friday for Robinson Crusoe, was never unduly impressed by all this prestige and magnificence. The Bourgeoisie would like to believe that it is a case of jealousy, but jealousy cannot exist without some degree of admiration, and this people of ours obviously do not admire it. In fact they make fun of it ; not of its greatness and power, but because it has no real sense of authority, nor the requisite manner, though always aping it. They make fun of it in the same tone of voice, with the same good-humoured insolence, as that old hated rival, the aristocrat, the nobleman . . . Please don't demur. You must have seen many men of our people but perhaps never properly, at those rare, precious moments when a man gives himself away. And—if I may say so—I doubt whether you have seen many authentic " *grands seigneurs* ", men of old France, primarily because the species has become very rare. Otherwise you would not be tempted to smile when I assert that a truly bourgeois bourgeois is as out of place, as inconguous, in a real cottage as in a real château, that in both places he suffers from the same inferiority complex and the same kind of embarrassment, though his manner is different. It is this inferiority complex which has gradually poisoned the relations between our bourgeoisie and the people from which it sprang and to which it is still so intimately bound : because of its pig-headed insistence upon playing a part far too exacting for its resource of mind, heart and generosity. It would like to be the people's honoured and respected guardian, whereas in fact it draws from the people its own well-being, fighting tooth and nail, relentlessly, not for íts privileges, but for its money : begrudging even the meagre wage it pays. The bourgeoisie has only gradually become aware of its false position, and far from making it amenable to the requisite sacrifices, this discovery has, on the contrary, terribly hardened it— at the precise moment when our people were recovering not the feeling for their rights—which they had never lost—but consciousness of those rights. I mean the rights which they owe not only to certain rules of equity, valid for all, not only to the principles laid down once more in the encyclical *Rerum Novarum*, but to birth, and History, and centuries-old service to the nation. Do you see ? Bourgeois econo- mists always argue as though our proletariat had been imported from another continent at the beginning of the industrial and capitalistic era, the only problem being to find it a suitable *modus vivendi*. This line of thought might be useful for Mr. Ford in dealing with his Polish, Czech, Russian, German and Hungarian workmen. But French workmen are not immigrants, after all. In the land of France, they are in their own home. In the history of France, they are where they belong.

When I speak about my people like this, I may astonish some Englishmen. I am not surprised. I myself took some time to reach the conclusions I am now setting out. For years the bourgeoisie has been conducting a campaign of slander against the people. In every campaign of the sort, there is some truth, some falsehood ; one can only judge with full knowledge of the interests involved. The treason committed against my country on June 10, 1940, and cynically perservered in ever since, under the protection of German bayonets, rids me of all doubt : the interests in this case were the interests of the enemy.

Such an assertion on my part will, I fear, never profit me in this world. Those whom I indict will never forgive me ; those whom I defend will not understand me, or will understand me at cross purposes, and will always end by preferring some platform orator or communist petty bourgeois. No matter ; I am performing a duty. The truth which I set out can be no more than a partial truth, but I give it as I know it. In the midst of the concert of lies, in the vast whirlpool of rival propagandas, I decided long ago that I would reduce problems to their essential, human elements, and try to solve them humanly, that is, according to reason, justice and honour. In saying that our bourgeoisie was incapable of playing an adequate part as regards our people, I have not, up till now, anyhow, charged it with a crime : I even took pains to analyse the causes coldly and impartially. But having gone so far, it is no longer enough to say that this artificial, hybrid class, born of economic circumstances, was inferior in quality to the one of which it claimed to be works' manager and director of conscience. The bourgeoisie has not only failed through ignorance, or egoism, to understand the interests which it set itself up to protect ; it has betrayed them. Anyone is free to write as he likes about our social conflicts. It is nonetheless true that the day has come when one side, carried away by hate and fear, has broken the national covenant and used the enemy against the nation. However ill-defined the problem was, nothing will ever justify the wretches who turned to Hitler and said : " Settle it for us ! "

What interests me in this fearful tragedy is not treason so much as the complex psychology of treason. What interests me is not the fact that our élites betrayed, but that they did so with a clear conscience. O Englishmen, Englishmen, Christian Englishmen, never forget this : the universal danger is not the dimming but the hardening of consciences. You all stood there, watching from your window, anxiously waiting, watching the men of disorder, pillage and arson, without the least air of suspecting for an instant that while the men of disorder were what they always have been, it was the decent people who little by little, imperceptibly, were shifting, changing. As they were all changing together, this was not self-evident. And you had no wish to see it. Obviously it is difficult to say at what precise instant the change started, but such transformations can usually be detected in the way men talk. Now I believe I may safely state that our bourgeoisie began to betray, more or less consciously, when it started talking morals and Christianity.

This is not a joke, nor a paradox. Such talk was not natural to it. Throughout the nineteenth century, our upper middle class spoke another language, at the furthest pole from Christianity ; it was the positive language of economists and business men, as unsentimental as could be ; it was the language of realism. " What ! " people will say : " are you accusing the materialist Voltairian bourgeois of the days of Louis Philippe of becoming idealist ? " Hold on a moment ! He has not become an idealist ; but for public use he has adopted the idealist's vocabulary : it is not the same thing. And moreover—please note— they do not even take the trouble to hide their game : they say they are more realist than ever, more realist than their grandparents, for it is clear that Louis Philippe's bourgeoisie would never have gone to Munich ! These men use Christian terms to serve their interests and their prestige. Of course—let me repeat—no formula is supple enough to cover so many-sided a case of conscience. For nearly a century the bourgeoisie had nursed the almost complete illusion of its sovereign right, and the basis of its right it found in the principles of liberal economics ; social inequality, even carried to extreme injustice, was one of the necessities of competition, and competition was the law of Progress. Of what relative importance was the destitution and death of millions of workers, compared with the increase of production which in the end would bring the world salvation ? With History and Science always on its side, where was the need for Morals or Religion ? It firmly believed its only opponents were workmen put up to the job and sentimental ideologists. And along came Karl Marx, by an inexorable bill of particulars condemning it precisely in the name of Science and History. But the Church in turn condemned Marx's materialism, and Marx's materialism conveniently drew attention away from the materialism of liberal economics. Why should the bourgeoisie not have rallied wholesale to the Church ? The moral prestige it was in danger of losing was restored to it by the once-detested priests, and they did it for nothing, or next to nothing, for it willingly left the matter of principles to the clergy, so long as it was allowed to interpret them in practice in its own way. Once he had read the Encyclical *Rerum Novarum*, you surely don't picture the poor dear parish priest proceeding to investigate the conditions of work in the factory of his wealthiest parishioner ? .But these priests, so intransigent about definitions, so accommodating about interpretation, gave the bour- geoisie an even greater boon : a quiet conscience, just when it was beginning to prick. What did the accusations come to, in fact ? The mere abuse of the Right of Property. But the Right of Property itself was what the other side was daring to attack. In the defence of this sacred Right, the bourgeoisie now found itself—the materialist bourgeoisie—at the side of the world's greatest spiritual power, it became its rampart against those " powers of subversion " denounced in all the utterances of the episcopate : it seemed to take up the inherit-ance of the Holy Roman Empire.   Could it ever have hoped, in an earlier day, that History and Science would be made to support it so advantageously and honourably ?

Until 1918, the bourgeoisie may have had its doubts concerning the authenticity of its apostolic mission ; but the coming of communism definitely marked it out—if I may speak thus, from a heart full of bitterness—as the true Eldest Daughter of the Church.   From time to time I have accused the bourgeoisie of using Catholicism rather than serving it, and that formula also is too simple.   The rally to what it calls the Church of Order was certainly more or less feigned, as far as the fathers were concerned, but the sons really did bring it about. There are thousands and thousands of young French Catholic bourgeois, for whom the Church is substantially nothing but a magnificent organisation.   This magnificence exalts them, as it exalted Maurras, and they take exaltation for Faith.   They understand more or less the essential distinction between the Body and the Soul of the Church, but this distinction strikes them as something recondite, a refinement, belonging to the part of " *counsel* ", not of " *precept.*"   Perhaps, as sound realists, they prefer to belong to the body rather than to the soul ?   The vast propaganda inspired, controlled, and organized throughout the world by the Jesuit Fathers is careful not to confirm them in this error ; but, in accordance with the spirit of their Society, they leave slightly ajar—*ad majorem Dei gloriam*—the door through which come to them so many powerful allies.   " After all," the reverend Fathers think, " if the good Lord, who nevertheless wishes only to be loved, deigns to make use of the fear of Hell, why should not the fear of revolution supply us with recruits ?   Once they are absorbed into one of our innumerable sodalities, it will be time enough to set them straight.   Until then, let us not disturb their honest faith."   What the reverend Fathers do not see, or pretend not to see, is that such an equivocation cannot pass without appalling injustice to the French proletariat.   It is obviously regrettable that our workers should in the end have entrusted the handling of their claims to marxist lawyers. But at the outset, had they entrusted them to the Jesuits, what would they have gained in the last fifty years ?   When, before 1888, the State recognized for workers no right of organisation or association, where were the reverend Fathers ?   Moreover, the reverend Fathers would have declined the honour, and not without reason.   So what could they do ?   Does a bad solicitor prove that a cause is bad ?   This time, it did.   In France the workers' cause found itself discredited, in ill repute, thrown out of court.   At every claim of the proletariat, legitimate or not, the " right-thinking " bourgeoisie with one voice conjured up the ogre of bolshevism. An increase in pay, a mere reduction in the hours of work, constituted a threat to the family, religion, morality and the Church. The bourgeoisie had ceased merely to defend its own interests long ago ; it was now the defender of the whole of civilization—a sacred cause. The old misunderstanding changed to hate, and even this hate took on a sacred character. Far more than this—the unpopularity of the " right-thinking " party having constantly grown, its rancour, exasperated by stinging disappointments at the polls, turned little by little against France herself. France was made responsible for the set-backs. It was France who would not understand or listen, France whose daily lesson Mr. Charles Maurras heard, and she did not remember even the a b c of it ; France, the idiot, the silly, stubborn fool. To be sure, for fifty years the ecclesiastic, eyes cast heavenward, deplored our ungodliness ; the moralist, our licentiousness ; the statistician, our sloth in procreation ; the doctor, our drunkenness ;—for fifty years the " right-thinking " press produced nothing but a surly bill of particulars against my country. They talked about France like teachers, and true enough, they were schoolteachers—not leaders nor guides—schoolteachers, embittered schoolteachers. They had got their knife into France— that is a fact—like a stepmother with the child of a former marriage ; and, like the stepmother, they justified their cruelty by asserting that the brat was naturally vicious and unmanageable. Nonetheless they found a way to manage it. They gave it a tough master with whom there is no trifling about behaviour and work : they apprenticed it to Hitler.

English friends, I hope you will read to the last line this small defence of the people of my country, before you throw it into the fire. I do not condone their faults. I maintain that behind any trouble that arises will almost always be found hypocrisy and imposture. Thus, throughout the last century, it was the upper or middle bourgeoisie, the peasant proprietors, who, in order to avoid the apportionment of estates required under the Civil Code, practised the theory of the " only son." In those days the poor—poor devils—reproduced like rabbits, despite a horrifying infant mortality, in certain working-class regions of the North and East as high as 77 per cent. It is odd, surely, that that furious campaign of books, articles, pamphlets, speeches, sermons and episcopal commands against birth control awaited for its unleashing the moment when the workers tired of producing children for institutions and cemeteries, and so threatened a decrease of man power and an increase of wages. It is odd to hear marshals and generals to-day preaching homilies on the insufficient French birth-rate, when nobody was asking them to reproduce themselves, but definitely to produce tanks and planes.

I do not condone the faults of my people. I assert that their masters have not understood them, and have never really tried to understand

them. I do not say, either, that the masters' principles were wrong.
I say they did not know their job as educators.   If your child, obviously
gifted by nature, becomes a dunce at school, you don't start reforming
the masters ; you change the school.   But nations can't change their
masters like that.   The masters of my people were not masters at all,
just hack teachers ; bitter, disgruntled schoolteachers.   They did not
love my people, they were too afraid to love them.   They insisted on
treating them like savages, Calibans, whereas they were merely children
with bad manners, of high parentage.   They wanted to purge them,
that is, to suppress their liveliest traits ; and this is a typical school-
teacher's wish, his ideal good pupil being the docile, passive, studious
dunce, the incurable mediocrity, the failure-to-be.   I do not say these
things lightly : have these masters given themselves away, since, or
not ?   Have they, or have they not, since then, shown a people
nourished a thousand years on honour, that they didn't give a damn
for its honour, and preferred their own security to the honour of the
people ?

Perhaps even this formula is still too summary and unjust.   I want
you in England to know how much I wish those fellows were altogether
worthless : the future of my country would then seem less gloomy.   An
unworthy member is like a dead limb ; it only needs amputating.   But
they are still fastened to France by living ligaments ; they cannot be
torn off without running the risk of grievously wounding France in her
own body.   For months I have been watching treason as a surgeon
watches a cancer.   For months ? No.   For years. I have seen the tumour
grow.   It spreads wide and deep.   The hatred of our élites for the
people is not a simple feeling, yet I must call it by the right name of
hatred ; I can find no other.   It is an almost unconscious feeling, a
social and herd reaction, analogous to religious hatreds.   Every single
German—man or woman—could not, without injustice, be considered
personally capable of committing the crimes of the Gestapo.   And
many people cannot bear the sight of a surgical operation ; but the
idea of it does not revolt them—quite the contrary, if they judge the
operation useful.   In Majorca I knew some society women who for
years, in order to acquire merit in Heaven, visited poor working-class
homes and took an interest in their lot.   When the purge began, they
did not for a moment dream of blaming the executioners who came to
slaughter their quondam protégés in their own houses.   Our élites
began to hate the people almost without knowing it, on the day they
despaired of it ; and I can put my finger on that day : it was in May,
1923, that famous " black Sunday," disappointing all the hopes which
defeat was to fulfill but not till seventeen years later.   What ! less
than four years after the Armistice, those incorrigible masses were
voting " Left."   Once again the people were eluding them !   Had
they been worthy of their name, they would have undertaken serious
self-examination, with a view to reforming themselves and at all cost
remaining in contact with a people exhausted by war and disgusted

with the peace. They should have tried somehow to understand this exhaustion and disgust. But they lacked precisely the most indispensable virtue of élites, the sense of responsibility in command. Here we had subaltern élites, capable of getting orders carried out, not of giving them ; they were intermediaries. What might have been a dramatic social development of world-wide significance, their mediocrity reduced to the level of a family squabble ; and these are usually the most hypocritical and atrocious of quarrels, poisoned as they are by the money question. Our bourgeoisie did not forgive the war for having impoverished it, that is, for having assailed it in the most tender spot of its prestige. It felt ridiculous in the eyes of the poor devils, to whom its economists had promised wealth with victory for four long years ; and it did not dare admit its failure. Towards this proletariat, so eager for social reform, it had the same resentful feelings as a business man towards an employee who elects to ask for a rise on the day when a large note falls due. Still more, it resented its budding sympathy with Russia, whose bankruptcy had recently brought to light many a secret hoard. In the long run, the hatred of Russia has perhaps become doctrinal hatred ; but at the outset it was, I assure you, a positive, practical, stolid hatred—a stolid hatred of thrifty men caught out in their calculations, and creditors spurned by the debtor. The collapse of the Russian loans, coincident with communist propaganda, was a fact of considerable social effect among us. It dug a deep rift between the petty bourgeoisie and the working class ; it pushed the petty bourgeoisie into the arms of the greater bourgeoisie. The stranger in our midst exploited this misapprehension with advantage.

From now on, I can safely say, the damage was irreparable. When I speak of the enemy within, I make no distinction between soviet and totalitarian propaganda ; both strove for the same object : they wished to create opposition between the two halves of the French people. And nothing can convict me of error in this because my findings are based upon a handful of concrete facts and clear evidence. I shall not commit the injustice of coupling the working masses and the élites together as though they were equally responsible for the ruin of my country, and as though responsibility were not to be assessed with due regard to dignity, status and function. To hate those in command is a low-down feeling, though a very natural one. But to hate what is below one betrays an ignoble perversion of heart and mind. I accuse the French élites of having acted treasonably. But I accuse them even more of having in their treason compromised, perhaps beyond repair, a good infinitely more precious than themselves : the very principles they claim to uphold and without which they are nothing.

I say that this treason dates from long ago. The crime of the French élites is nothing like what the criminologists call blood-crimes. It was not an act of blind violence. All the evidence goes to show that they came to it slowly. This precisely is what constitutes their guilt. When a man of high standards is involved in evil-doing, he cannot let himself go completely without violence to his nature. So first he cheats himself a little and plays with the notion, though still convinced he is rejecting it ; and so his conscience gets used to it. Then he finds it excuses and justifications, still pretending to believe he is far from the deed itself : he weighs up the risks, telling himself that such calculations are quite gratuitous and will lead to nothing. But chiefly he keeps in mind, and gets others to bring to mind, the worthlessness of his opponent, whose death he already desires, though he does not yet intend to carry it out himself. Such precisely has been the role of the so-called National Press. Till the day its paper crumbles into dust, it will remain an unimpeachable witness. To anyone familiar with the history of the French press, the thing appears as a unique phenomenon, though the Anglo-Saxon public, for instance, may find it difficult to see it in this light, used as it has been for so long to methods altogether different. At first it was, de facto and de lege, the utterance of a small minority of Frenchmen, so unimportant that even to-day, in a France thoroughly demoralised by defeat, it can only cling to power with great difficulty and with the help of German bayonets. It remains none the less true that such a minority was once able, in a short space of time, to absorb rival publications and drown all other voices. Abroad, in Brazil as elsewhere, it was taken to be speaking in the name of France, it was French public opinion. Unable to create a France in their image and likeness, the future leaders of the New Order presented the world with a sham France, so that in due course they might pose as liberators of a phantom and a fiction, while they clamped real France into irons.

I know that such explanations repel the average reader. What the average reader wants is average explanations with a soothing effect on the mind. You all forget that my country's disaster filled you with horror ; why should you not find the causes horrifying too ? If the event was an unprecedented scandal, do you hope that I can without scandal indict those responsible for it ? Of this gigantic press, I assert that those who launched it, at great expense, could have no direct expectations for themselves, or for the success of their cause by legal means. The rumblings of this enormous machine were sufficient to deafen the world, but it could not have shifted fifteen hundred French votes ; I even say that it would have cost its promoters the most striking of their electoral setbacks. Hence it was not French opinion that they hoped to reach. By slandering my country under the hypocritical pretence of defending her against herself, by declaring her a breeding place of revolution, a menace to the order of Europe, they were preparing world-wide opinion for the catastrophe, they were making it seem inevitable ; and once a catastrophe seems inevitable, it is not far from seeming well-deserved. By their agency, millions of our friends, in every latitude, especially in conservative and religious circles, dared no longer say " Long live France ! " They bowed their heads and murmured " Poor France ! "

Years before Vichy, the spirit of Vichy, the spirit of bowing to fate, of resignation, of expiation, of Vichy, was thus spread throughout the world, creating an atmosphere appropriate to our coming failure. True enough, such an attitude of contemptuous pity earned them, within the nation, growing unpopularity ; but the wretches did not let this disturb them, they no longer worried about adversaries whose score seemed to them settled in advance by the inevitable triumph of fascism in Europe. Oh, of course you will tell me that the bulk of their docile following were more or less unaware of such schemes. The shame of that public lies in its never having seriously wished to see clearly ; its crime lies in its half-wilful blindness. It did suspect that its press was sold to the enemy, but it hoped never to be faced with the proof of the transaction. " They may have been bought, but after all they are defending us against the Leftists ", such was the answer given by many decent people, magistrates and priests.

Supposing that in about 1930, you English readers of mine had made the following remark to one of the men I am speaking of : " Your workers are quite unbearable. After all, what would you have to fear now from an Italian victory ? The Duce's army, navy, airforce are irresistable ; your fate would be settled in a fortnight, and without heavy losses . . . Pride apart, moreover, a defeat would suit you better than a victory ; it might perhaps cost you Tunisia, but Mussolini would soon bring your noisy brawlers to book. And then, good-bye to demands for social reform ! " The man you were addressing would doubtless have appeared a little uncomfortable but he would in the end have answered with a shrug : " Those accursed workers would certainly have earned what they got ! " Three or four years later, however, Mussolini was no longer in the running ; the unanimous outcry of civil, military and clerical Rightist circles was, " Rather Hitler than Blum ! "

I want you to realise in England how little the outside world knew of these dramatic events ; the news of the rout of France came like a thunderbolt. The world as a whole knew nothing about us, because it got its opinions from writers who played in our society the part of valets and chambermaids in classical comedy : they throve on the vices of their masters. That Mr. Winston Churchill could have wasted five minutes on Maurois is a disconcerting fact. As for me, I bear witness of what I saw. I saw the conscience of our élites grow corrupt. I might write some well-turned sentences on the corruptors ; I prefer to call your attention to the corrupt, for the corruptors were in the service of the corrupt ; they furnished them with arguments and excuses. Whenever Philip the Fair was planning some political trickery, or rather as soon as he decided on it, he ordered his jurisconsults to justify it in advance in the name of Justice, and his chaplains and his casuists to justify it in the name of Morality. This is how the French ruling classes acted, though of course less openly. Maurras was its jurisconsult. It cared precisely nothing for the theses of " integral nationalism ", in which it had never seen more than an intellectual pastime. Of this neo-patriotism it wanted only the underlying principle, the " all means are good " which had been its rule in business deals for a long time—" business is business "—but which it had never dared publicly to proclaim. Maurras freed it of its shyness. Realist in business, liberal and even idealist in politics ; at last the contradiction could be discarded which had cost it so much trouble, and brought it not the least success at the poll : the legacy of 1848 could be discarded once and for all, as well as that sentimental chauvinism, so far removed from its nature, of which it was ashamed, which it found " plebeian ", and which indeed was of the *plebs*. What was more, Maurras allowed it, by a.subtle dodge, to revert to the old bourgeois theme of " peace at any price " born of our history's only truly bourgeois government, the monarchy of Louis-Philippe. Post-war pacifism at first appalled it, for the same reason that it fired the popular imagination. It never expected peace to set the world free, but hoped—at least before the disappointment over Germany's bankruptcy—that peace would allow it to strike the war off its books and replenish its funds . . . This it thought, without daring to say. M. Maurras said it for it in highly dignified terms. And it began to shout : " Long live Peace ! " whereas by these three words it meant, " Down with taking chances ! "

This is not just my point of view. I shall repeat as often as necessary that there are many ways of premeditating a crime ; the first is to tune one's mind to it and make one's conscience agree. The proof that our élites had premeditated their crime is not the fact of our downfall, it is that once the disaster had taken place, they immediately found themselves at home in it. Not only was the policy of defeat ready at hand, but ready also—carefully done to a turn—was the casuistry necessary to justify it. Everything which goes by the name of Right, extending from the alleged monarchists of the Action Française to the allegedly " national " Radical-Socialists—big industry, big business, the higher clergy, the Academies, the general staffs—spontaneously gathered and agglomerated upon my country's disaster, like a swarm of bees around its queen. I do not say that they intended this disaster, by a deliberate act of will. They expected it. This monstrous readiness is what condemns them.

They expected it ; they were ready. For twelve months now they have given themselves away day by day. What they say publicly to-day, they then said to one another. Marshal Pétain's homilies do no more than repeat the conversation, in Madrid drawing rooms, of this both proud and fearstruck greybeard, during the days when he already represented, among Spanish fascists, not France, but the Contrition, the Expiation of France. France entered the war with her élites won over to the idea of defeat, of an " expiatory defeat "—as though a defeat accepted in advance had ever been able to redeem anyone ! Such an accusation scandalises you because you never see anything anywhere but axioms and formulae—never men. The men I speak of were too deeply compromised to draw back. Then as now, the triumph of totalitarianism in Europe was for them the only way out, for ever since the rise of Mussolini, they had always put their money on fascism, each time doubling their bets. They were totally the prisoners of this doubling system. How could they have longed for a day to come when their case would come up before the nation !

As I have already said, the so-called National Press—their Press—will remain overwhelming testimony against them : *scripta manent*. Whoever without prejudice undertakes to comb through this vast mass of files, will have to yield to evidence : the so-called National Press has always, everywhere, and on every occasion, served the interests of the Foreigner. Of course, almost to the very end, it preserved an anti-German tone ! I ask all readers of good faith : what else could it have done ? Did it not stop the moment it could ? Would Hitler himself have wanted a premature excess of zeal ? Germany was duly reviled. On occasion, stern measures were demanded. Only because they were known to be impracticable, or easily made so. There were theoretical justifications of measures which could only have been put into practice at the risk of war, and the nation was passionately dissuaded from such risks. German might was a fact. But they boosted Italian might too : they kept the public in constant terror of the invincible fascist fleet, which could swallow the English fleet at a single gulp. Do you make a nation ready for supreme sacrifice by proving its powerlessness day after day and by overwhelming it with a sense of frustration ? These unspeakable wretches were saying that the totalitarians wanted war, right into 1938 ; but once Czechoslovakia had been crushed and Germany was ready, they threw their mask aside ; they began to say that it was the democracies which wanted war by order of the Jewish international. They became anti-Semitic, because they had had their instructions. To be perfectly frank, I have never believed in the sincerity of Hitler's anti-Semitism. Hitler has made use of anti-Semitism, as of anti-communism, to corrupt European opinion, divide it, disunify it, provide the nations who were to be his victims with grounds for civil war. In due course he will re-incorporate his Jews and recognise the Jewish banks ; he will make it a German national institution, and we shall see a novel and startling form of Kollaboration.

All the so-called National Press campaigns have been profitable to the enemy ; eliminating the chances of victory, moving step by step towards defeat. This could be proved mathematically ; the campaign against the League of Nations, a masterpiece of hypocrisy, for by feigning to brand its weak points, it weakened it still further and made its impotence absolute. The campaign against American war debts soon turned into one of slander against the American people, whose sympathies Hitler was anxious to alienate from us. The campaign against China, fobbed off as communist. The campaign against " masonic " Czechoslovakia. The campaign against the Russian alliance, the Russian army, the Russian air force. The campaign in favour of collaboration with Italy against Germany, a crafty variation of the campaign against the alliance with Britain ; the military bankruptcy of fascism has proved the absurdity of this, but it gave Hitler the advantage of embroiling us with our Balkan allies at just the right moment. The campaign against Ethiopia and sanctions, which dealt the final blow to the Geneva League, and so gravely compromised the prestige of the English fleet in the Mediterranean. The campaign in favour ·of Spanish fascism, when the success of General Franco was indispensable to Mussolini's security in the Mediterranean. Finally, and chronologically the last, that furious, delirious crusade of 1939 on behalf of Finland, which galvanised with enthusiasm all the Kollaborator drawing-rooms of Paris, all the gilded rabble of defeat, and which had no other purpose than to achieve the irreparable—a declaration of war between England and Russia and the final throwing of Stalin into Hitler's arms.

The Masters of the so-called National Press had evidently sold themselves to Germany, but the real proprietor remained in the background, to spare their feelings : they dealt only with his agent, Mussolini. The masters of the Press had sold themselves and their public was not aware of it. Mussolini was keeper of consciences. He had taken over the national conscience and had given a receipt for it. I could supply the name of a writer from the best bourgeois circles who, wishing to acquire a daily newspaper, found it quite natural to have the funds provided by the Duce. He admitted it himself, with no sense of shame. And when I reported the fact to a woman worthy of all respect too, I expected an explosion of wrath, or at least an expression of incredulity, but she just said : " What of it ? The others go to Stalin, and it's for the wrong cause. Where else do you want our people to go ? "

One day, these people will say Mussolini took them in. Maybe. Such an assertion will not save them from punishment. They had had time to think. The wholesale purchase of " right-thinking " consciences had in fact begun about 1932. It is probable that for the moment Hitler still hoped to deal with us decisively by means of civil war not unlike the Spanish war, which would have opened the way for the intervention of brown shirts and black shirts. He spent huge sums of money to bring this about. He had the cash, but he lacked the men. He had taken seriously gangs of brawlers, fully determined not to come out into the open except under the cover of his bayonets. Doriot spoke ; Maurras wrote ; the first was a man of wind, the second a man of ink. I shall not do the others the honour of recording their names. As for the clerical choir boys, the darlings of the Reverend Fathers, they were, as usual, resolved to wait comfortably at home while the enemies of Society were exterminated, reserving their energies for the thanksgiving processions . . . Disappointed of his hope for civil war, in September 1939, Hitler certainly looked for a *coup d'etat* on the part of the Right wing opponents of war, with the reversal of our alliances and the installation of the French New Order ten months earlier. So he might have been spared the expenses of a campaign and the risk of a tardy awakening of the national spirit after the humiliation of defeat. But the Kollaboration crowd were too decrepit to pour out their own soup ; it had to be brought up to them in bed. The German army had to go all the way to Bordeaux.

August, 1941

I REALISE I could have painted quite a different picture of our troubles. I should have had no difficulty in finding authorities and describing the interplay of characters like the old-fashioned historians : but I want you in England to see that here, precisely, it is the characters that are missing ; perhaps you have already begun to notice that the play is anonymous. It all goes on in the wings, the stage is empty ; one would have to fill it with supernumeraries, with " walkers-on." Marshal Pétain is himself merely a supernumerary, a walker-on, a poor devil. These people have spent all their lives in Opposition, that is, in a state of perpetual criticism and censure : " They should have done this . . . they should have done that . . ." And if they can do something positive now, it is because France is helpless. They refuse to see it ; they try to reassure one another ; they tell one another that their principles are beyond reproach, drawn from the best sources, and approved by the teachers and the priests. The principles are valid ; it is they who are worthless. They are doing what they have always done : defining, not acting. Were the principles a hundred times better, they would dishonour them just the same by seeking to foist them on a conquered, prostrate nation without even the strength to spit in their faces. They rape France while she is in a coma, and expect a child to be born alive. Alas! what was lacking was not good principles but men capable of serving them.

The story of our terrible misfortune is a very ordinary one, a common and almost trivial story. It is a story of treason with no traitors, enormous with consequence ; yet look at it closely, and it splits and shatters into an almost infinite, incalculable number of sordid trifles : as though all the mediocrity which, when spread abroad in this great body, did not threaten its vital equilibrium, had suddenly gathered at one point in a huge, fixed abcess. The satanic genius of Hitler's propaganda achieved this masterly stroke. It ferreted out a handful of half-true, half-false notions suitable for cementing together all the mediocrities; it federated them. The mediocre soldier, the mediocre intellectual, the mediocre priest, who sometimes thought themselves so far distant from each other, suddenly realised that they were closely linked together, bound by their common mediocrity. And the cohesion of the mediocre made any national reaction impossible.

We must not allow ourselves to be deluded by the mediocrity of
the protagonists as to the real meaning of the event and the lesson
to be learnt from it. The mediocrity which got the better of my
country has not yet spent its venom ; it still flows in the bloodstream
of all nations, it can suddenly strike heart or brain and cause the
same lightning paralysis. Applied to your particular case, the
hypothesis strikes you English as absurd. But you are waging war ;
you are right in the thick of it, whereas this time, we French never
came in . . . War accelerates a nation's circulation prodigiously and
burns away all waste products all the time. So long as your men are
fighting and dying, you have no need to fear the formation of a cold
abcess . . . But if the spirit of Munich had won the day in England
in June, 1940, you too would have fallen into the same hands. Cursed
world, that cannot ever escape the clutches of the old and purify
itself of the spirit of old age, but at the cost of a huge libation of young
blood !

In my last letter to England, I said how bad this world was for
childhood. It isn't much good for nations, either, for nations are children
themselves. You often say so, but perhaps you don't give the words
the same meaning as I do. For many people, Marshal Pétain, for
instance, they mean that nations are not capable of looking after
themselves, and that they have to be made happy in spite of themselves, with a bludgeon if necessary, all for their own good . . . How
many of you reading these pages will at this point take off your spec-
tacles and say, " By Jove, how true that is ! " Put your glasses on
again, and to Hell with you ! They never will be masters : they are
servants become masters ; they speak on behalf of slaves, not for
children or nations. You cannot make a human being happy in spite
of himself ; you cannot, in spite of himself, make a man happy, any
more than you can make him a hero or a Saint. But it is true, nevertheless, that nations and children need happiness above all else. We
make the same idiotic mistakes with nations as self-centred bachelors
with children. We want them to be happy with what rouses our own
envy. But is there anything more difficult to satisfy than a child ?
By what mystery does the little girl prefer to all the beautiful costly
dolls, her shapeless dolly ? Or the little boy, a limbless lead soldier
to all his expensive, instructive mechanical toys ? By telling themselves that nations are children, the fools regain self-confidence,
whereas they should tremble. They mistake the child for the urchin :
the most generous go no further than wishing nations enough to fill
their bellies. Is this not an absurd way to treat noble old nations like
the French and English. Are these beggar-nations ? But the Bourgeoisie measures them by comparison with itself : it attributes to
them its own fear of risk, taste for thrift and passion for comfort.
Whereas nations and children love risk, and don't mind at all about
thrift and comfort. Is this just my opinion, or does History prove it ?

I say History does—the most ancient as well as the most modern—
for, after all, it was not by filling her belly that Hitler made Germany
fanatical. The élites deplore that the nation no longer understands
them. But it is not the nation's job to understand them : it is for
them to make their intentions clear. Anyone who sets up to be an
educator stands self-condemned when he complains he is neither
respected, believed, nor loved.

English friends, I am almost alone to-day in bearing witness for my
people ; I may be the last to do so. If God does not grant you victory,
who will save it from a slavery a thousand times worse than material
slavery : who will save its soul ? Its freedom lost, who will save its
soul from losing the spirit of freedom too ? The most precious possessions, won at so heavy a cost, are enjoyed by my people without their
knowing it ; and they have only their instinct to warn them of the
danger which threatens. Quite capable of dying generously to defend
them, they cannot describe them or even give them a name. If their
own élites betray them, how will they be able to stand up to the
schemings of foreign élites and the prestige of enemy cultures, German,
Spanish, Italian, working in concert for the same end, though by
different means ? Indeed, no nation can boast of owing nothing to
others. Our national culture has by turn come under various in-
fluences, which have left visible traces ; these are the weak points
where the poison seeps in before reaching the nerve and locomotory
centres. The traitors know what they are doing when they extoll
the spirit of expiation and humiliation ! Once the French élites are
out of the running, gone over to the conqueror, the enemy have nothing
to fear from our people but a blind, brutal retort of national pride.
By overwhelming it with the memory of its sins, they deprive it of
its last chance and deliver it over, numbed and bemused, to the new
masters.

Our misfortune may some day be yours. Victories are worthless in
themselves ; one has to know what will come out of them, for there
are sterile victories, and the most brilliant of them are not always
the most fruitful. Your British victory must make the world human
again. This word *human* can, I know, have many meanings. But we
are not discussing a kind of abstract humanity ; we are talking about
humanity living, suffering, dying under our eyes, about the humanity
of that small peninsula, Europe, where most of us will leave our bones :
and that humanity is Christian. Whether one likes it or not, such it
is. Those who deny it seem to me less dangerous than those who
agree too readily without thinking, perhaps even without really
believing what they state, just because the statement gratifies and
reassures them. It is however neither gratifying nor reassuring. True
enough, to a great number of fools, Christian humanity means above
all a tractable humanity, easily governed and controlled, well held in
check by the priests, admirably disposed never to disturb the rich in

the quiet enjoyment of the good things of this world, all in return for
a promise—a conditional promise, too—of beatitude in the life to
come. No, I mean a humanity informed by Christianity, which means
a humanity whose moral actions are dictated by that thousand-year-
old atavism, and that is what no one will take the trouble to understand.

The people no longer go to Mass or listen to sermons ; they don't
know their catechism ; but the image they bear within them, deep in
their very souls, without knowing it, is of a society which never
actually existed, but for whose unbelievable advent their ancestors
waited, century after century : the city of true accord, under the
seal of brotherhood. You will naturally answer that these are very
personal views, and I understand your feeling tired of talk about
Christianity and Christendom ; the young whipper-snappers of neo-
Catholic literature have worn you out already. But these are not at
all personal views. Were you to take the trouble, at a restaurant or
public house or factory, to listen for five minutes to French workmen
whom you suppose to be communists, discussing what is just and
what is not, you would admit that the conscience of these fellows is
far more difficult to satisfy than that of a Greek or Roman freed man,
or even of an ancient Hebrew . . . And society, as conceived by
your bankers, engineers, economists and moralists, will never, never
satisfy them. They will say it is because they don't get enough
money, and they work too hard ; you will accuse them of being
insatiable, and they will agree, they will even cynically boast of it ;
but if they don't feel at ease in this society, it is because they do not
find it just—without quite knowing why—it doesn't suit them, that's
all, they don't feel at home. Once more : I am speaking of your
people or mine, two old nations. I am not standing up for Mr. Henry
Ford's labour gangs.

For these men, a human world must be built up again, of the same
kind of humanity as their own ; for these men, a Christian world
must be built up again. This does not merely mean a world, alas !
where those who to-day dub themselves Christians would be the masters.
Whether such Christians are truly Christians—looked upon as such
by God himself, I don't know. And how should I know, being quite
unable to say as much of my own self ? Who could claim to be
Christian, without being sure how he stood with Christ ? And who
dare claim to be the friend of Christ ? I have no objection to their
professing Christian doctrine ; that is their business and the business
of the theologians who instruct them. We are not dealing with a
theological problem, but with a social problem. To build up a Christian
society anew, is it enough to put it into the hands of the Christian
public, of average Christian opinion, of any who come forward calling
themselves Christians ? Certainly not. There are, of course, the
pastoral letters and the Encyclicals. I agree it is the doctrine of the
Church, and mine. But I am talking about men and the way they
apply these things ; that is my concern at present. Well then, the

Christian Society of average Christians—I know it only too well : General Franco is the model before me. That Society has not changed much during the last few centuries, and our Catholic Cromwells are very like your own. From the point of view of the social observer, whether heretics chop off the heads of Jesuits, or Jesuits burn heretics, the two facts are in the same class and the conclusions remain the same. I have said, time after time, that the Spanish Counter-Revolution in itself did not strike me as of great importance. The immense, capital fact is that average Christian opinion identified itself with that Counter-Revolution, and almost unanimously conceded that the proper retort to massacres was not the just punishment of the murderers, but the systematic extermination of the opposition, the " wrong-thinkers " and suspects. By approving the purge system, with which they were already familiar, seeing it in use long ago in Moscow, Rome and Berlin, the majority of average Christians in all countries, both the pastors and the faithful, have solemnly foresworn the dispensations, exemptions and immunities due to the pacific nature of the true apostolate. Well, it is their look-out. They oppose force with force, and on the assumption that their opponents have placed themselves outside the law, they do likewise, and follow them into that region, that no man's land, the more freely to pay off old scores, and for no better reason. This is how they propose to go on fulfilling their duties towards Order and Society. But wait a minute ; I shall not allow them to trifle with words. Christian Order ? Christian Society ? No. Neither this Society nor this Order are Christian ; I base my assertion on evidence which is unimpeachable, as many of them know and as I know. The Church does not recognise this Society and Order as Christian. The pious may say what they like, but the Church says what it means, and this doctrinal infallibility, which for so many implies the enslavement of consciences, is precisely what frees our consciences. It protects us from the tyranny of shifting opinion and local distortions of the Christian intention, placing at our disposal, at mine, now, an immemorial, unchangeable, imperishable tradition ; so absorbing in its prejudices, passions, interests and politics that the Popes themselves might be tempted to turn aside, did they not know that the whole tradition is at stake every time they speak. It is not we who are bound by doctrinal infallibility ; it is that infallibility which holds the living Church in chains, to stand or to fall by each decision made : all or nothing.

Neither that Society nor that Order are Christian. From Pius IX to Pius XII, the Popes have not ceased repeating this. Need we say it too ? If Christian society and Christian order were to result in the monstrous squandering of immense production, by which speculators alone grow rich and the poor stew in their own poverty—and then in a general war, far more monstrous still, since, literally and precisely, it would bring civilisation to the edge of the abyss—there would be nothing for it but to despair of Christianity. I may be told

that society is not responsible for these catastrophes, but the forces
of evil. Well, but is it not specifically Society's job to guard us against
the forces of evil, and keep us in wholesome fear of them ? Society
requires of each of us two-thirds of our goods, and when we pay this
enormous insurance premium, it declares itself unable to carry out
the contract, and puts a gun in our hands so that we may do it ourselves.

No doubt the Christians I am talking of dare not publicly assert
that it is a Christian society, but in practice they act as though it
were, they identify themselves with it, they place outside human and
divine law those whom it has driven to despair and delivered over to
all the temptations of despair, through the scandalous impotence of
its inherent contradictions. When they are accused, they whine
and say that such a Society has never meant more to them than a
Lesser Evil ; on that account, they guarantee it provisionally and
conditionally, and will denounce it the moment it falls ; they always
have ready at hand and filled to the brim Pontius Pilate's basin of
water. They do not understand, they will not understand, that a
society unable to do its job, and sweeping its members into fearful
catastrophe, can be maintained only by force. They call themselves
pillars of Society ; they are in fact the tools of Force. They bring
Force a support infinitely more precious than their craven hearts and
their feeble arms—the prestige of a doctrine which they say they
follow, and of the Church whose champions they claim to be. That
was their way in Italy, Germany and Spain. And if it was not their
way in Russia, though Pius XI had shown them a score of times the
basic identity of system and methods, they say themselves it was
because Russian totalitarianism is a more open, if not more direct
menace to Property. Of all the admirable structure of ancient
Christianity they are reduced to defending only this last bastion :
the only one for which the disciples of the Poorest of the poor have
sworn to fight till they die under its ruins ; it seems to them a thousand
times more precious than Freedom, Justice and Honour. " We are
not defending property," they say, " but the Principle." Here again
we shall not allow them to trifle with words. In its conception of
property, Modern Society has not the slightest connection with
Christian Law : it has gone back to the traditional forms of the
implacable Roman Law. For under Christian Law, the proprietor is
the steward of what he possesses ; he administers it for his own profit,
of course, but also for the welfare of the community ; he is responsible
to the community. Christian Law never recognised the " right of
abuse " which allows speculators, large or small, deliberately to
destroy precious necessary commodities to keep prices up ; so the
principle, the famous Principle of Property, rallying all the Really
Nice People, the People of Worth, " Hombres dignos", that principle
you so proudly emblazon on the banners of the Crusade, is not even
Christian. " We know it," they reply ; " we defend it conditionally,
to keep the worst from happening." Of course, you take it for a

relative truth—am I not right ? How unfortunate that you are not seen treating with relative severity those who question or deny it. You agree that they should be shot ; if necessary, you would lend a hand.

Pharisees ! Vipers ! You avenge crimes against Order, Christian or not, with a machine-gun ; to denounce crimes against Justice, all you do is to write pamphlets in such abstruse terms that your victims are left in the dark. You fight for property-owners with lead, and for the poor and destitute with paper. Hypocrites ! I have so far hesitated to speak like this because I feared—not your reprisals, God knows !—but your slander, *et a verbo aspero*. But now I have grown old, my work is done ; there is probably not a blockhead in all the world capable of believing that the author of *La Joie* and the *Diary of a Country Priest* is planning a career as a demogogue. Heartless, witless Christians, I have always, since my young days, looked you straight in the face, with a sort of despairing curiosity, for I can frankly say to-day that you were an intolerable scandal to my childhood, an obsession I was able to shake off only by trying hard to understand you. You are the scandal of the Church, yet it must needs be that this scandal remain ; so Christ would elude our reason, our judgement, our very conscience ; only the heart seeks Him and finds Him there ; you are the sacramental species of the Sacrament of Sacred and lasting Humiliation ! Ah, well. Such ideas can only interest a very small handful of readers, and I apologise for them and for that slight outburst of scorn. Scorn does me no good ; it invariably accompanies a fit of depression. And I have noticed that indignation has, on the people I am discussing, merely the effect of inflating their pride beyond all bounds, and I do not want to contribute to the hardening of their hearts. " Well then, stop talking about them ! " you may exclaim. I fear that such a topic will not win your good graces, but I am not writing for that.

English friends, let me tell you that it is a fatal mistake to under-estimate the mediocre ; mediocrity is a colourless odourless gas : allow it to accumulate undisturbed, and suddenly it explodes with a force beyond belief. Many of you are utterly uninterested in the future of Christianity and will find these pages tedious indeed. Others have eyes only for the external and material signs of decay ; every Sunday they count on their fingers the numbers of parishioners present at the sermon. But the dire omen for all of us—yes, for all of us, believers or unbelievers—is not fewer Christians, but the increasing number of mediocre Christians. You may think mediocre Christians are nothing to worry over, but the power they can still wield is enormous. All the learned academies of the Universe could solemnly convene for the purpose of promulgating a new morality ; the moment it emerged from their crucibles, this intellectual elixir would at once begin to lose its potency . . . Whereas these millions of Christian men and

women, were they even more degenerate than they are, would have a
real and unquestionable right to a morality so familiar, for centuries,
to all consciences that it has indeed become our conscience ; nor is
that all ; it has worked down into our subconscious ; it may be said
to inform our instincts, it has become morality incarnate.

I know its precepts are recorded in learned tomes, and that the
charity which gives it life beats on in a certain number of predestined
hearts. But all these pious conformists, scattered throughout a
world which you regard with indifference or irony, if they cannot
prevail against the precepts, may well in the long run invalidate their
practical application. If I may use another metaphor, these people
do not possess the source of the river, but they securely control its
flow. To a believer like myself, this fact has not the importance it
should have in the eyes of unbelievers. No citizen in his senses, were
he utterly unacquainted with religious dogma, could, without dis-
composure, watch a certain species of men influencing almost the
sum total of consciences through their hold on most of the vocabulary
of morality. The smallest concession on the part of average Christian
opinion can have consequences of terrible gravity for society and
culture. Is not such concession the great danger to-day, threatening
as it does to put the genius of France, heir of Hellenic civilisation, at
the mercies of an inhuman humanism ? You are constantly being told,
in the interests of propaganda, that a return to Christian principles
would save the world, and the maxims of the Gospels are quoted as
proof. But principles, by themselves, can save no one ; principles
do not save without men. It seems to me more accurate to say that,
shifting to a certain angle, and with a certain degree of adulteration,
good principles are much more likely to wreck the world than bad.
Believe me or not. I do not ask you to adopt my faith. It is in the
interests of the societies now threatened that I beg them to see the
danger where it really is, not in the subversion of the Forces of Evil,
but in the corruption of the Forces of Good. Whether you like it or
not, there is nothing better than Christian morality to oppose to the
new moralities ; and you would be wrong to think the new can put up
nothing valid against the Christian, as though the maxims of God
were Euclidean axioms. No, in many ways, the doctrine of the Gospels
is a paradox and a challenge ; and in old times, so it was seen. The
sacredness of the human person is a more difficult thesis to maintain
than its opposite, the absolute dependence of the individual on the
community. It appears that in Germany they are beginning to get
rid of the infirm and weak-minded by means of euthanasia. For the
same reasons, one might also destroy many other less seriously damaged
goods, if likely to cost Society more than they bring in. An analogous
train of thought might lead to the suppression of a certain proportion
of the poor, especially those with a long family inheritance of poverty
and little likelihood of being able, through their own resources, to
better their lot. After all, this kind of purge of the down-and-outs is

as justifiable as the purge of those with the Wrong Ideas. If you were not Christians, if the blood of ancient Christianity did not run in your veins, it would no more shock your conscience than the murder of a slave would have disturbed a citizen of Rome or Carthage. And if all you oppose to this ferocious logic is merely the Letter of the Gospel, dear friends, you are beaten from the start. The Devil is the greatest of logicians ; there is no logic like the logic of Hell.

You must expect no help from the Letter. The Spirit alone can save you. Believers or unbelievers, every weakening of the Christian spirit is a catastrophe for each one of you. We must stand together to meet the peril which threatens us all ; we shall be saved or perish together. The word *charity* may not have a very clear meaning for many of you ; never mind. Every particle of Christ's divine charity is to-day more precious for your security—for *your* security, I say —than all the paper securities in the coffers of the Bank of England. Without it, the Christian masses, seemingly so obedient to their pastors—you see them marching in serried ranks at Eucharistic Congresses—would not be of much use to you in times of trouble. What is visible is nothing, less than nothing, a coarse dough where you see no leaven. Your eyes are all for the young toughs, the church wardens, notabilities, band and drum. You may notice the richly adorned canopy, like a banner, with its plumes and fringes. That too is nothing. Under the canopy is a minute white host, quite invisible from where you are sitting. So far so good. Don't expect me to expand into soul-stirring, heart-touching periods at this point ; what I think of what is a thousand times dearer to me than life itself does not concern you ; I haven't the least intention of converting or edifying you ; I merely hope to make myself clear to any reasonable man, that is, anyone capable of accepting in good faith the results of experience.

So we have this minute host. And then, here and there, hidden away in the great crowd, are people whom you are certainly not likely to notice : timid old priests, men, women, little children—good, or not so good, no one minds. You will not find them among those who turn up the whites of their eyes and put out their tongues in seeming ecstasy. What their hearts hold rarely shows in their faces, they do not even know what they have in their hearts ; God alone knows. Between the white host and these human creatures, so uninteresting to the spectator or the camera, there is mysterious intercourse. This is what matters ; I beg to assure you that it is as I say. However you may explain the fact, there it is, evident, as it has always been evident throughout the centuries. The moment danger looms, not over the treasures of the Church or its dignities, but over its Faith, the poor insignificant wretches I speak of become martyrs—you know this as well as I do. They quietly say, No ! to Powers to whom they still humbly paid their respects only yesterday ; and, moreover, their " No " is as humble as was the respect they paid, but implacable, unyielding, inexorable. The gentle obstinacy of these predestinate souls has caused more blood to flow—their own blood—than all the pride of conquerors. And what is more surprising—account for it as you will—the coarse dough of which they were the leaven then begins to work. The bigoted become forgiving and charitable ; the miserly become prodigal ; the casuists become simple as little children ; the cautious gladly take risks ; political prelates lose their guile ; and tyrants, masters of palaces and basilicas paved in gold, are suddenly dumbfounded, anguished, terrified, to hear the old Church, her youth renewed, singing in the depths of the Catacombs.

I beg your pardon ! You may object to this lyric strain—and I am not in any case appealing to the poet in you. I might just as well have said quite simply that Christianity only shows its full strength when under trial. Adversity does not make it strong, but it does set everyone in his proper place, with the saints in front. So I have the right to conclude that if you are perfectly entitled to use the Church to help you face the doom which threatens the world—the Church is at the service of all ; it contemplates with Mary, but is not too proud to give soup to the poor with Martha—there is no need to wish it persecution to make it holy—this would hardly be charitable—but it is absolutely necessary for you to wish heroes and saints for it. It is true that the Church is a great temporal power. You eagerly tot up its adherents, organisations for propaganda, newspapers, avowed or secret political activities, and immense resources. All this is, of course, not negligible ; but you always will price it too high and make a bad bargain. Whoever tries to use the Church for realistic ends, in a realistic spirit, always gets the worst of it. Precisely to the extent that you think to secure it to yourselves by clever deals, you detach it from what constitutes its real power. I repeat, this is not a question of idealism but of experience. The clerical factions in our country never had more powerful means at their disposal than during the last years before the outbreak of the war. They had a hand in everything, as they say. And what a lot of hands ! The forthcoming liquidation of their childish national revolution will show you that I was right not to stake a penny on their chances.

I quite understand the logic of the realist politician. He is not proposing to found a Christian society ; he just expects Christians to defend his society. He assumes that the millions of parishioners wearing blue, yellow, green and red ribbons in the Jesuit Fathers' groups will make excellent recruits. Friends ! What a mistake ! The specifically human value of these parishioners is very much lower than you reckon. Let me once more inform you that a mediocre Christian is a poor sort of fellow, generally inferior to any given un-believer of similar standing, for he is a living contradiction of the truth he professes, and he can only solve such a contradiction by casuistry and imposture. You count upon him to defend our society, and he makes a similar reasoning ; he counts on your society to defend him. You are taking one another in because each of you hopes to give much less than he will receive. In short, collaboration with the Church is for the realist a Last Resort, whereas collaboration with the realists is for the Church a Lesser Evil. And this is one of the most bitterly comic scenes History has ever staged.

At last I am coming to the end of my long message to England. I send it to you like the others, from the depths of my solitude. And in speaking to you, I speak to my own folk too ; I can trust only you, who are free, to transmit it to the remaining free men of my country. If I were living among you, perhaps I should not have dared to write it. For pages and pages now, my subject has carried me further than I would have gone on my own accord, but what is written shall remain written ; I shall not go back on it. You have not been reading a bill of particulars, or a brief, or any formal document. But if I am not to survive my nation's disaster long enough to see the day of justice dawn, at least you will have heard the dying sigh of a French conscience. In England, in the secret hope of reassuring yourselves about the future, you would perhaps dearly like to believe that this world-wide distress is the work of a small number of individuals, as political and worldly chit-chat constantly reports. Or else, as the oracles in prophetic guise would have it, that it has deep moral causes, so deep that then and there you judge it useless to accompany these gentlemen in their profound investigations. Personally, I am sick of learned dissertations larded with terms which mean nothing to ordinary people and create the illusion that the fate of the world is determined nowadays in philosophic congresses.

Please will you listen, Englishmen, to the appeal of a simple man, who owes his modicum of insight to loyalty and love alone. Do not pity France ! " I want none of your pity," she will tell you, " not because it humiliates me, but because it puts you in danger of going astray." Don't think that pity absolves you from further concern with this major disaster : it is a lesson that must be learned in England. As long as I live I shall repeat that the blame for my country's moral defeat must be laid on those who were the natural guardians of its conscience, and the proof that they failed is that we see them cynically exploiting that failure to their own profit. The same breed of men will, to-morrow, exploit your victory. Suppose that a miracle, or some unforeseeable event—the stroke of genius of a military leader, a technical discovery, or anything else—had given us the victory last year ; those same so-called " national " élites, those " right-thinking " bourgeois, generals, admirals, members of the Academy and Archbishops who to-day would have us see in Hitler the providential instrument for avenging them, would be strutting about panoplied in our honour, just as they now strut panoplied in our shame. For the last months, the leaders of the democracies have constantly been talking of Christian principles. Let them mistrust principles ! Our élites had principles, they crawled with principles as a corpse with maggots.

Do not be surprised at a Catholic speaking to you in such terms, it is precisely because I am a Catholic that I do so. My Church is the Church of the Saints. The cult of the Saints shocks many of you, who believe them prisoners of the Church. But it is the Church which is their royal prisoner. Living, they gave everything. Dead, they make it a living tradition, they are its witnesses and judges. It was a mere pastime for the Doctors of the Law, Scribes and Pharisees, to overwhelm Jeanne d'Arc with their dialectic. But they are dead, whereas their victim is still alive, truly alive, irrefutably endowed with life and honour. To-day she is much more embarrassing to their eminences Cardinals Baudrillard and Gerlier than she would have been of old, at Rouen ; I need not tell you why. To the least sentence spoken by this child of Lorraine, obstinate like all her race, this small page boy of the Lord, as bold as a page boy, indeed, dare one say it, cheeky, whose every action and every word were a challenge to the Wise, Prudent and Wary, we now find the Wisest of the Wise, the most wary of the Wary—I mean the Churchmen—attaching a supernatural, doctrinal value, through a solemn, irrevocable promotion; to the least sentence from her lips which the clerks of the Tribunal have transmitted to us down the centuries. Not that she was learned enough, poor girl, to define such words as *Patrie*, Honour, Oath, Just War ; but the Doctors who undertake such definitions to-day cannot avoid writing as though in her presence, under the same proud, innocent, slightly mocking gaze with which she once faced her judges. Do you understand ? Now, those of us who would venture certain justifications of defeatism, basing them on the still mysterious words of the Gospel, " Those who live by the sword shall perish by the sword ", should first start the Rouen trials all over again, and they can no longer do it. Our Church is the Church of the Saints.

To Englishmen and Americans, Christians of the Reformed Religion, I say, it is true our Church looks like any other Human institution from a distance ; old age and the spirit of old age appear as powerful there as elsewhere. Make no mistake. It is in fact the only one where Childhood is not the ward of Old Age, but where the Aged are the wards of the Children. It is a very moving thought that to-day even, when my country's Church is yielding more than ever to the cold speculations of senile prudence, it holds in highest honour two young girls—Saint Joan of Arc and Saint Theresa of Lisieux.

Letter to the Americans

September, 1941

TOWARDS the end of one of my books, *Les Grands Cimetières sous la Lune*, called in English, *A Diary of my Times* I allowed myself to speak to Hitler in familiar terms. Why should I not speak to Mr. Roosevelt now ? I do it all the more readily because this new inoffensive monologue is not much more likely to reach the ear of my illustrious interlocutor than the first. Dear Mr. Roosevelt, I would say to him. You will surely have been pleased to learn in 1938, that the American bishops were calling all Catholics to a Crusade on behalf of Christian Democracy. This was quite an important affair at the time, but taken all in all, it did not seem to me more important than the call of the Spanish hierarchy to the Phalangist Crusade. These great events are unfortunately beyond the scope of a humble writer like myself. Since the advent of Mussolini, I have heard so much talk of Crusades that the word has lost some of its magic as far as I am concerned. You will not be angry if I tell you that Crusades interest me less than Crusaders, for, strictly speaking, one could imagine Crusaders without a Crusade, whereas one cannot conceive a Crusade without Crusaders. Is the American episcopate sure of its crusaders ? I apologise for asking this question. I should not do so if the Italian, Spanish or German hierarchies were to make a like appeal for the same cause ; those who responded would certainly be heroes. Dear Mr. Roosevelt, I greatly fear that on this side of the Atlantic such an act would have all the appearances of a declaration of loyalty toward established institutions, or what you might call an intellectual mobilisation. My illustrious friend, Jacques Maritain, has just founded in London, with Christopher Dawson, under the presidency of Cardinal Hinsley, a monthly paper of a similar temper : *The Sword of the Spirit*. It is not the intellect that is sick, but Conscience. And a sick conscience gets on very well with its illness ; it is in no hurry to be cured, it refuses to consult medical books or tries to have them put on the Index.

If, after two thousand years of Christianity, it still required all the learning of the doctors to declare that two and two make four, that is, that no one is free to perjure himself, or to shoot down innocent people, or to solve the Jewish problem—*and there is one*—by exterminating the Jews, or to open up new trade outlets by means of hyperite or mustard gas, we should have to despair of Christianity. To speak in this connection of misapprehension, equivocation or clarification, seems to me a proof of sheer insolence. Dear Mr. Roosevelt, believe me, when the Church becomes too political, it is due to

its no longer producing enough saints ; just as a sick man develops
eczema for lack of exercise. Dear Mr. Roosevelt, you are perfectly
right in thinking that God has chosen your nation to make the final
decision as to the fate of Christianity, and that soon. It is a great
honour, but it is also a great responsibility to be appointed by Providence testamentary executor for the dead, for those who formerly
perished in such a cause were not of your blood nor of your land. Now,
when the will of the American nation is preparing to tip the scales,
let me tell you that you are backed by their countless sacrifices, as
well as by all the gold of the world. Never has any nation run such
a risk, supernaturally, as yours is about to face. It must save Christian
civilisation, or perish with it, with every possibility of being damned,
for there is no forgiveness for betraying the Spirit.

Dear Mr. Roosevelt, you yourself belong to the Reformed Religion,
but you know that ever since the first Christmas night, one name is
common to all Christians : men of good will. You are a man of good
will. Furthermore you have power and genius. Your calling of
American opinion to order can justly stand as a masterpiece of reflection
and intuition, a work of art of irreproachable proportions and a model
of style, if style is expression perfectly adapted to subject matter. In
many ways, your nation remains unknown to us Frenchmen, but your
particular genius is of a kind which we now understand very well—
passionate and lucid, sensitive and practical. The coarse-grained
Germans reprehend its feminine traits, as they do ours. They do
exist. The women of your lineage must have been noble women, like
those whom we honour and to whom our race owes so much. From
a man like you, the savage *a priorism* of a German heart or brain is
not to be expected. You certainly have no hope of setting Christian
civilisation on its feet again without the Church, or against the Church.
It is equally true that the greatness, power, and temporal efficiency of
this collossal Institution may be something of an offence to the
Protestant conscience. We know all too well the mistakes, faults or
even crimes that are imputed to it. If, in all the elements of which it
is composed, its power was always all for Good, the kingdom of God
would be here now and the petition in " Our Father " answered.
Its mistakes are the price paid for Power. And this temporal Power
is no longer ordered according to Justice and Charity, when the
temporal Masters of the World seek in one way or another to involve
it in their schemes, and to control men's consciences by means of it.
Any such scheme is idiotic, if I may say so, Mr. Roosevelt. That is
how Spain once became the terror and laughing stock of Europe.
Kings, Emperors and Republics naïvely believe they have got the
Church under control, when all they have got is some miserable
specimens of mankind. All Churches have their conformists, but it is
natural that the most scandalous of all should be the conformists of
the Church whose divine Founder deigned to institute the reign of

Grace in place of the reign of Law, and was, indeed, crucified by the conformists of His own day.

Dear Mr. Roosevelt, with the weakening of Christianity there immediately appear in large numbers those people whom Pius XI described as " spiritual individualists," bent on working out their salvation by themselves, and extending to the salvation of others only as much solicitude as they think necessary to further their own. The Christian faith is not, for them, an engagement for life, a risk to be taken, but the same form of security as that given by an insurance company on the material plane. They guard it as jealously as their worldly goods, they are as proud of it as of a presentation gift, a decoration or a title. They live in terror of losing it, and their sub-missiveness to the pastors is much less like that of a soldier who follows his leader under fire than a sick, obsessed man's blind confidence in his doctor.

Dear Mr. Roosevelt, people who would have you believe that the world will be saved by such folk are just being funny. They have quite enough to do to keep themselves going, with all their countless societies for relief and mutual assistance to keep them in frail health from the cradle to the grave. But do not believe that they are merely harmless. It is not generally realised that it is a wavering faith which turns to fanaticism : and, given the opportunity, the mediocre do not hesitate a second to make unbelievers pay dearly for their own uncertainty. It is an easy way of convincing themselves that they love their Church as much as they hate her enemies. Dear Mr. Roosevelt, there are many decent folk among them, but as I have already had the honour of saying, nothing is more dangerous to deal with than the consciences of decent men, once they are warped. Ever since you and Mr. Churchill began to talk of truly restoring Christian values, they have been extremely lively, they believe that they them-selves are those values . . . The moment your democracies are victorious, you will see them rushing up in crowds. Nothing will equal the zeal of the Christian of Rome, Berlin, Madrid ; they will put the Christian democracies of England and America to shame. Dear Mr. Roosevelt, please do not think that the poor priests, monks, nuns and young sisters who, with great concern, shepherd these deceptive flocks, are responsible for this painful comedy. Some few of them obviously delude themselves as to the value of their lambs, and congratulate themselves when they seem so plump and spruce and woolly, but this is a perfectly natural feeling. They shepherd the flock and get nothing for it. Those who exploit the flock, exploit its mediocrity, prejudices, prepossessions, mistakes and fears are precisely the very ones—or their counterparts—whom to-day you see so busy in France ; politicians, journalists, ambitious women, intel-lectual misfits, embittered bourgeois, obtuse military men, scheming monks, diplomatic and political monsignori. They it is who control average Catholic opinion, and that opinion is worth nothing ; less than nothing ; its only use has been to provide an excuse for lucrative bargaining, profitable collaboration and expensive rallies. The exploiters of mediocrity ordinarily work in secret, but by the will of God—I hope—my country's misfortune has brought them out into the open. They are as visible as a colony of microbes projected on the screen in a documentary film.

Dear Mr. Roosevelt, when the time comes, I know what this sort of people will say : " We do not actually claim to be Christendom, but our powerful organisations do express the average opinion of European Christianity ; we are therefore the most fit people to collaborate with the statesmen. Of course we honour heroes and saints. Unfortunately, saints and heroes do not go in for politics. So we are essential. We did indeed compromise ourselves a little with Mussolini and Franco, for the simple reason that Discipline must be maintained ; this is the watchword for our programme. But the word Freedom is there too, and on that ground we can come to terms with you."

Dear Mr. Roosevelt, this is how I should like you to answer them : " Leaders of Christian opinion in Old Europe, we have been watching you for years, and, to speak frankly, although a large number of you lent more or less open support to Hitler's New Order, we regretfully note that you too often combine somewhat cynical courses of action, obviously inspired by the dictatorships, with the very spirit of hypocrisy and compromise of which you were so recently accusing the Democracies. You readily take us Americans for irresponsible and acquisitive people. We are less mercenary than we seem, and you are infinitely more so than you admit. The example you have given in France is in singular contrast to your pre-war statements, and it merely confirms the unfavourable conclusions which we had drawn from the Spanish civil war. You boasted of being traditionalists, and you accused us of lacking tradition. We suspected you of being more conservative than traditionalist, and you now prove yourselves to be, first and foremost, self-preservers. Gentlemen, I thank you for your offer, but I have no need of you. Why should I trouble to secure your services ? I know that so long as I remain powerful, they are mine for the asking. In a dying society like the one that has recently given way, you could, on occasion, be of some service, by prolonging ambiguous situations which were not necessarily harmful when they delayed a crisis which the world was not yet able to cope with. But now that is over. We have not sacrificed millions of men only to end in compromise. Oh ! I don't doubt you will say the Revolution still threatens and the Powers of Disorder have not laid down their arms. True enough. If need be, our reborn society will have to defend itself by force. But our police force is complete, and we have no need of you as auxiliary policeman. You would like me at least to authorise a public manifestation of your sympathy with the police ? There is no need. The police can perform their duties without the support of your plaudits. If not to the police, then it is

to the threatened property holders you would like to tender your
concern ? So you believe that without your moral support they would
come to doubt their own rights ? I think your fears are vain. Time
and time again, the Catholic Church has defined Property according
to Christian Law. Your excess of zeal would be more likely to confuse
a problem of human morality already magnificently solved, by making
simple people think the defence of the property-owner necessarily
entails the defence of the Right of Property. But those who abuse the
Right of Property do it no less harm than those who deny it outright.
We know that there exists a vast army of Disorder, ready at any
moment to put the blame for our faults and injustices on Society,
without which no civilisation is thinkable. And among those wretches
there are an indeterminate number who are beyond persuasion and
permanently estranged. But since the Society we know has, twice
within twenty years, engendered frightful wars, it is permissable to
consider that it may have been no more successful in solving the
problem of Poverty than that of Peace. Hence I conclude that we
should not despair of restoring to order, by means of Justice, those
unhappy masses whom your boasted dictators and leaders of Crusades
sought to exterminate through police action and discriminatory legislation. This should be possible for us in America. It should be even
more possible for you in Europe, the cradle of Christianity. You say
that the masses have become dechristianised. To what extent is this
true ? Which is the more Christian : an honest Paris worker who has
no knowledge of the catechism but is horrified at the use of poison
gas in Ethiopia, or the church-going Italian who approves it ?

" Let us leave it at that. The cradle of Christianity has nearly
become its sepulchre. Europe is an object of scandal ; the scandal
must come to an end. The miracle of faith, heroism and love which
the Church formerly brought about—can it be renewed ? It is a sad
duty for the heads of Christian States that they must, on occasion,
defend order at all cost, even against miserable, misguided wretches
whom we pity from the bottom of our hearts. At such times, I do
not consider that your place is at our side ; your support is rather a
hindrance. It is very fine to render to Cæsar the thing that are
Cæsar's but, please, not so much hurry ; wait till Cæsar asks for his
due ! We do not wish you to be compromised on our behalf, for once
too deeply involved with the masters, what mission can we entrust to
you on behalf of the slaves ? No one can make it his business to exhort
poor devils to resignation, submission and patience in humiliation
and injustice in the name of the Lord, and then publicly approve
their being shot down the moment they fail to practise these virtues—
heroic ones beyond the reach of many an ecclesiastic—and place us
under the sad necessity of answering violence with violence. In such
a case you would serve us far better, and far more effectively serve
order and the State, even preserving us from some dangerous nonsense,
if you would tear the weapons from our hands.

" Gentlemen, we are going to try to found a Christian society, that
is, a society based upon the Christian notions of Equality, Liberty,
Fraternity. That does not mean that it will be perfect—far from it !
Indeed we can see very clearly from the outset what will be lacking.
So don't burden us with the intemperance of your praise ! Don't
exult ! Don't seek revenge ! Don't prepare to settle down too
comfortably ! Don't beat the drums too loud for penitential processions ! You would seriously embarrass our labours, and even more
those of your Catholic brothers, the workers in the hive where you are
the drones. For your noisy advertising, alternately insolent and
servile, your clamorous, ostentatious dealings with party leaders and
governments—which have no other purpose, ultimately, than to cheer
on your ever-fearful flock of followers—are such as to turn the hearts
of poor people against the true apostles. You will say that in Europe
we must beware of a fresh bout of anti-clericalism. On this side of
the Atlantic, we have no very clear notion of the words *clericalism* and
anti-clericalism. Nevertheless we undertsand them well enough to
assure you that they are two sides of the same coin—the same vice in
mind and heart. Where the clerical waxes fat, the anti-clerical waxes
fat likewise. But I am ashamed to mention such silliness in considering the immense task that awaits all Christians. We do not ask
them to line up respectfully behind us ; we implore them to go ahead
and show us the way. We have no need for twaddle about legitimate
distinctions between Liberty and license, relative and absolute Justice,
courage and temerity, wastefulness and generosity. There is no
excess of liberty, justice, heroism and generosity looming on any
horizon. Human Societies are all too prone to sacrifice the promises
of the future to the security of the present and to think they have
reached their goal before they have started. Is it not shameful to
hear so many Christians urging us not only to prudence, but to that
shabby humanism, stuffed to the gills with history and experience,
babbling incessantly that nothing changes and there is nothing new
under the sun ? We had thought that Christ came to bring to the
world a principle of renewal which, endowing every man with the
means to outgrow his own nature, must endow the nations likewise.
You were of the same opinion ? Then why the devil do you act as
as though you did not believe it ? You give the impression of organising
everything so as to be able to do without saints and heroes. I am not
qualified to teach you better, but, judging at least by France's downfall,
your powerful organisations, which cost you so much trouble in
connivings, concessions and money, do not seem particularly to have
favoured, not so much the emergence of saints—that is God's affair—
but at least the natural output of heroes. So I remain somewhat
dubious. One of the most tiresome requirements of our profession—as
leaders of nations—is that we must make use of the mediocre. But
mediocre Christians, my dear Sirs, are too hard to fit anywhere ;
or rather, they have no place ; they are like great Lords fallen from

high estate, apt neither as chieftains nor subalterns. Instead of
bragging to me about the advantages of collaborating with you, make
up your minds, once and for all, to be either mediocre or Christian.
And when I ask this, Gentlemen, I am entitled, as the head of a State,
to do so. You obviously have a very out-of-date conception of that
function : you imagine a world divided between plebeians and
patricians. Loyal to schoolday memories, you evidently pin your
hopes on Sulla as against Marius. A single undisciplined action has
in your eyes more importance than a hundred abuses of power ; and
then, too, abuses of power don't frighten you ; you openly boast of
preferring injustice to disorder. Unfortunately, Germany's example
has proved that the plebeian masses can easily become Sulla's hench-
men. We are beginning to understand that the general annihilation,
not only of liberties, but of the Spirit of Liberty would be the worst
disorder of all ; it would be absolute disorder under the guise of Order,
for such order would, in the precise meaning of the word, be inhuman.

" Dictators no longer face their people whip in hand ; they say to
them : ' We don't want to tamper with anything really useful to you ;
we only want to get a hold on your souls. Put up with us, just as
you put up with the other necessities of life ; do not dispute our
right ; let us judge of good and evil for you. Give us your soul, once
for all, and you will see at once that the cost is merely the sacrifice
of your self-esteem ; it was a burden beyond your powers, a ruinous
luxury. Forswear your soul, and so be quit of ruling yourself ; we
shall administer you like a capital investment, we shall make such
efficient stuff of you that you will be able to stand up to anything.
Men without consciences, gathered into colonies like termites, will
easily overcome the rest. The human animal, industrious and shrewd,
meticulously cross-bred by the best methods, will dispose in a single
mouthful of the poor dreamer formerly called moral man, foolish
enough to suffer countless trials for the hollow glory of being distinguished from the animals by virtue of qualities other than a higher
degree of cunning and cruelty. All the riches of the earth await those
who first commit themselves to the new path, and first forswear their
souls.' Gentlemen, there is now no point in discussing which is
preferable, injustice or disorder. The point is to save justice so that
order may be saved. In this final struggle, the people must be with
us. Then what is the good of men who are on such bad terms with
them ? If the people are ready to abandon the cause of justice, it is
because they no longer believe in Justice ; if they abandon the cause
of liberty, it is because they no longer believe in Liberty. You often
claim to be men of order. Now let yourselves be known instead as
men of justice and liberty, to become men of order again, when order
has been established in accordance with Justice and Liberty."

Dear Mr. Roosevelt, please forgive me for speaking in your name ;
I know that if you were to use such terms yourself you would run a
serious risk of disconcerting American Catholic opinion. I presume

that this opinion is powerful and has great resources at its disposal, as well as a technical organisation beyond reproach, fit to arouse the jealousy of rival communities. It is an excellent thing to pile up reserves, and your trans-atlantic Christendom may one day be the arsenal of European Christendoms, as your nation is already the arsenal of the Democracies. But arsenals are worthless without soldiers, and the last word in armament programmes lies with those who get killed. I fear American Catholics may have an American idea of the present condition' of Europe. They are most assuredly first-rate people, but they are used to seeing what can be done with money, and we are far better at knowing what can be done without any. They live in peace in a magnificent country almost the size of a continent, and the religious question must seem to them a problem not unlike those they have already solved. Unfortunately, the religious question is not merely a problem to solve, it is a dramatic action, the greatest of all, and sooner or later all are drawn into it. If love is not the theme, it will be hate ; and in shape and sequence it is unlike either politics or business. To-day Europe is deeply engaged in such action, and your turn is coming ; there is no point in having any illusions about it. American Catholics say the old continent is suffering from a fit of *delirium tremens*, like a drunkard breaking up the home. They will wait till its fit is over and then they will generously replace the broken crockery and, by way of comfort, will offer the sick man the example and lesson of their own prosperity. This is sheer illusion and profound error. There is many a ruin in Europe which a skilful administration will certainly be able to build up again. But consciences are not so easily repaired ! American Catholics, you may properly be proud of the religious peace you enjoy, which allows you quietly to grow in numbers and influence, in a spirit of fair-dealing and almost sportsmanlike competition with the other religious communities of Free America. Unfortunately, if you will think it over, this proves one thing only : skill in taking advantage of favourable circumstances. Here is nothing which can mend, or even palliate, the immense new world-wide scandal for which universal Christianity is responsible. For the real scandal is not the war ; it is the anarchy of Christian consciences which the war suddenly laid bare.

Blessed be the war for this, anyhow ; it has revealed it in time. Men had reached the point of thinking that definitions are all that matter, and it is enough to go on and on repeating the same phrases like parrots, to achieve a common soul. The ecclesiastics congratulated themselves on our discipline, and it is true that it made their relations with governments much easier, since it allowed them to guarantee our acceptance of any régime, once it was established. They said we were above politics and such crude temporal concerns, and that our communion in reverence and love for the same moral principles knows no frontiers. Unfortunately, when Politics set upon Morality to rape her, it was not to succour Morality that we all came running. Morality cried out most bitterly, but the Christians of Italy, Spain, Germany and even France pretended not to hear.

American Catholics, our scandal before the whole world is to have shown ourselves divided on questions of elementary morality; but the worst scandal was not the fact of being divided, but was, and still is, the ugly casuistry which explains and justifies it. American Catholics, that scandal must be cleared up; I even dare say that for the honour of God—there is such a thing as God's honour—it must be avenged. So long as it is neither made good nor expiated nor avenged, it will weigh upon you as it weighs upon us. Christians of America, more urgent than the pacifying of minds is the restoring of the dignity of conscience. We cannot quit ourselves of this by vague and pompous declarations, as though we had permission to turn up overnight as referees in a bankruptcy we are interested in not merely as creditors. If we are not affected by what is most hateful about it, we can at least see the ridiculous side. The other day Cardinal Hinsley publicly described Hitler's emblem as the " cross of the devil ". Italian or Spanish Cardinals, on the other hand, see in it the " in hoc signo " of the anti-communist crusade. Nothing could more clearly show the inability to distinguish between God and the Devil. American Christians, your answer is that you have loyally stood your ground on the side of the democracies. The exemplary value of this loyalty is gravely impaired by the fact that it is your country that is the greatest and richest democracy in the world . . . The unfriendly suggestion will be made that you have followed public opinion rather than pressing ahead of it, and when so many of you gloried in the Spanish totalitarian crusade, were you being particularly hostile to Mussolini or Hitler ? Your fans will no doubt have other things to say to you. That is not what matters. There has been the scandal of our division. There has been the scandal of the justification of our division. To-morrow there will be the scandal of our suddenly renewed unanimity at the victory of the democracies—with the chance of pointing out to all the poor devils our very odd ways of drawing the distinction at last, rather late in the day, between Good and Evil. Perhaps you still hope that, if the scandal is not made good, it can be covered over after the war by doubling, tripling, increasing tenfold the number of school, post-school, pre-school, educative, protective, recreational and corporative good works, for you have by you the means to set afoot an immense scheme for the provision of spiritual armaments and supplies, of which the cost in dollars and cents can easily be reckoned beforehand. Dear American brothers, the nations have not got so short a memory; I fear the Revolution will be ahead of you . . . Routs are only ransomed by victories; sloth and cowardice, only by a surge of courage and boldness. That is how the scandal must be made good, with no time to lose, and in the very place where it is doing most harm : I mean in Europe.

Beware of Europe, Americans! You are too much inclined to believe that at the end of this horrible nightmare, old Europe will have exhausted all her spiritual reserves, and that you will merely need to pour in your own stock, just as you will generously supply wheat or potatoes. But it is not so. Nor is old Europe as old as that ; you are unduly impressed by a few extra centuries—a mere nothing ! Comparisons don't prove much, it is true, but I shall make my thought a little clearer by asking you to consider the fact that Chartres Cathedral, for instance, is in reality much younger, that is, more appropriate to young hearts and young minds, than many a monument which fifty years ago seemed to your millionaires the last word in modernism. Europe is not old ; it is the élites of Europe who need renewing, and who refuse, and now we are cluttered up with their remains. Beware of Europe, men of America ! You are young : I say Europe is, maybe, younger, certainly younger than you were in the days of the trusts. It is absurd to believe that nations go from childhood to old age, like animals, by a relentless progression. The spirit of age and the spirit of youth can be dominant turn and turn about, and if the spirit of age, that is, the spirit of avarice, rules too long, of what consequence is the actual number of centuries recorded in history's calendar ? Nations dry up, they perish ; torrents of blood shed too late will not set the sap coursing in dried-up tree-trunks. Beware of Europe, Americans ! The present crisis does not appear to be a crisis of senility. Old age is marked chiefly by diminished nervous energy. Europe's nervous potentiality remains huge. Don't imagine that all those folk are going to stay quiet just because to-morrow they will be drawing large salaries and living in comfort, with electric kitchens, central heating and a wireless set. Europe as a spiritual focus has been incomparable ; she will never renounce the rights she, justly or unjustly, claims to hold over the spiritual destiny of the world. I am speaking now of the people, not of governments or élites. The élites certainly have a much clearer notion of these rights. Only they don't care : they would readily sell them for a mess of pottage. The élites have kept the nominal rights and lost the tradition. The people have the tradition but no nominal rights. Don't get it into your heads that destitution has driven them mad ! That is what is said, they repeat what they hear and end by believing it ; obviously they are not accustomed to self-analysis. Our people may not know quite what they want ; but they want no more of a certain conception of life which it is not at all unjust to label " bourgeois". The people want no more camouflaged materialism, that materialism which defines and justifies itself by adapting to its own ends ethical and spiritual modes of speech, with a great number of Christians as its accomplices. They prefer misery and death to the insiduous mediocrity which is gradually spreading like mould over our civilisation, the mediocrity of the technical schools, and comfort, that ghastly void. The people of Europe prefer to die outright.

No doubt this is all very shocking, for we are used to treating the Bourgeoisie as an idealistic class—the very height of paradox—and the people as a pack of conscienceless brutes with only their bellies and their genitals to think of. Dear Mr. Roosevelt, you know that they are nothing of the sort, and your friend Winston Churchill is too great a gentleman to have been taken in by so crude a swindle. Our people are not mediocre. Our people never of their own accord turn to the mediocre solution, in Good or in Evil. If they become communists, it will be our fault, for they are quite unaware that Marxism springs from a materialist conception of history ; they do not give a tinker's damn for historical materialism ; they become communists exactly as the young French priests and nobles of the eighteenth century were set on fire by the Social Contract and Jean-Jacques Rousseau. It was in Jean-Jacques Rousseau's name that the enthusiastic young priests and nobles were finally beheaded ; it is in Karl Marx's name that Stalin's dictatorship has already caused rivers of workers' blood to flow. And our people still believe that they see in the hardest, most abstract, most intellectually dry political and social system, based on a frankly pessimistic conception of man and humanity, the very prototype of humanitarian religion, the Gospel of a new brotherhood.

Dear Mr. Roosevelt, there are some things that it is not easy for you, for all your genius, to understand from this side of the Atlantic, and besides, no one has ever told you of them. When you want information, for example, on Europe's religious crisis, a throng of nobodies and chatterboxes at once rushes up to break the news to you, or else honest priests, simple-minded religious, too busy doing good and too humble to have a personal opinion, naïvely repeat what the chatterboxes and the nobodies have just written in the clerical press. All these folk assure you that the peoples of Europe are becoming pagan. But wait a minute, Mr. Roosevelt. Through our own fault, our people are falling into a sort of religious and moral anarchy which does indeed put them at the disposal of any kind of revolution that may occur, communist or totalitarian. Paganism, however, is not anarchy ; on the contrary, paganism is Order of a kind, a very strict order, a relentless one which has already shown its mettle for centuries. Believe me, it is the élites who are becoming pagan, it is the élites who, while calling themselves more Christian than ever, are little by little rallying to the pagan order, to-day named " totalitarian". Now the Pagan Order was not without justice. Theirs obviously owes much more to Machiavelli and the rotten gangsters—titled or mitred—of the old Italian renaissance, than to the *Leges Corneliæ*, the *Leges Juliæ*, or even the Antonines and the Severi. Dear Mr. Roosevelt, the European élites may have to pay a high price for the scheme they had evolved for linking the cause of the Bourgeoisie to that of the Church. To ensure success, they worked on the quiet to reduce the social role of Christianity as far as might be, making Christianity a mere matter of self-discipline, a Morality ; a private Morality which in effect applies only to the individual pious bourgeois' relationship with his confessor. So strictly private is it that it is taken for granted—at least tacitly—that it has no claims on the politician or even the tradesman : politics are politics and business is business. . . . But the peoples remain attached to the old Christian tradition, dim though it has become. What do you think they make of the temperance societies, pious associations, devotional co-operatives and academies ? They do not know exactly what it is they lack, but they miss something. They miss that dream of their forefathers, of a great adventure, spiritual and temporal both at once : that great pilgrimage of Humanity towards the Golden Age of the Evangelical Beatitudes. How in the world could one persuade such men that the Lord only came to earth to prevent them from taking a drink too many on Sunday, or going to dances ?

Dear Mr. Roosevelt, I am no doctrinaire, and if I appear to be a literary man because I write books, I assure you it is merely an appearance. I am obliged to write books, but I should a thousand times prefer to dispense with publishers and booksellers and travel quietly along haphazard roads, talking about things I like with people I happen to meet in a stray inn, leaning on the table, looking them full in the face, and saying whatever came into my mind. But life is short and I am beginning to grow old ; you will agree that in that way I should waste a lot of time. Never mind. But remember you are not at the moment listening to a specialist in social, religious or political questions—a Thinker—but to an ordinary man from our continent, or rather from the centre and heart of it, for France is the centre and heart of Europe. Many a fool has said so before, I know ; but I am not ashamed to write it after them, because it is true. My country is the heart and conscience of Europe, which does not mean that it is better than the rest, but merely that it reacts more vigorously to good as well as to evil. It is the first to fall sick and the first to be cured.

Dear Mr. Roosevelt, I speak as any Frenchman would speak if he were free and spoke freely ; that is, if he were not unwittingly bound by prejudices of class and party and their jargon ; I snap my fingers at such things, and when you want to talk to the French, you must do so, too. You Anglo-Saxons do not understand how much the French hate the very lies they seem most attached to ! These lies are like hardened old mistresses : they have no idea how to get rid of them. The French love the truth, the French want to see clearly within themselves, and they will never hold against you the pain you cause them in tearing out a lie as a dentist drags out a tooth, for that tooth was an agony to them, even though they stubbornly refused to admit it.

Dear Mr. Roosevelt, if we want America to speak frankly to us, it is essential that we speak frankly to America; don't you agree? Mutual-admiration societies are useless. Europe has not finished her job, and your powerful nation has scarcely begun its own; I mean that it is just beginning to understand that the nations are jointly responsible to each other; and so far it has only covered the first lap, for it seems to think that such duties can be fulfilled by signing cheques. Mr. Roosevelt, if Europe does not save civilisation, it will destroy it; it will destroy all of you as well as itself; your fellow citizens should be clear about this. It will save civilisation only by renewing it. At the moment, does there exist in America a new, or renewed, form of Western civilisation? No. Yours is the perfect organisation for extracting the maximum comfort and profit from a civilisation which you naïvely supposed able to make ephemeral things eternal, and whose destiny you expected to work itself out far away from your own boundaries. You have had to let this consoling illusion go, for now you perceive that the well of water which separates you from us does not make it possible for you to go on quietly with your experiments.

Dear Mr. Roosevelt, Europe has to reconstruct its spiritual unity. It is the fashionable slogan of the day, and everybody uses it without understanding it. If you do not want it to re-discover its unity in communism, there is little time to waste, I assure you. You pride yourselves, you Anglo-Saxons, on being more or less refractory to communism. You also believe that it is merely a reaction against certain economic phenomena which can probably be side-tracked, and that a policy of high wages will easily hold it at bay. I wonder whether you are not mistaken. The communist intellectuals naturally exploit the mistakes and contradictions of a declining society; but the communist intellectuals are one thing and communism is another. Do let us get this clear! For years now, both on the right and on the left, intellectuals the world over agree that " things can't go on like this . . ." They write it in verse and in prose, colloquially or with pathos, ironically and seriously, in sacred style and in profane. So we cannot exactly blame the people for expecting something new. They are used to manual labour; they know its rules, they live in its traditions; they do not like to make new things out of old materials and they despise patchwork. If you wanted to go on patching up your Modern Democracy indefinitely, you should have done it on the quiet, and not have let them see what you were doing. Let's be fair! Twenty-five years ago we spent several million lives to put it back on an even keel, and the dead had not crumbled to dust before it was plucking at peoples' sleeve, and whining: " Things aren't going right; I need a little bit more fixing. Fix me up, won't you please . . ." The people quite naturally concluded that in mending the old machine they would spend ten times the cost of a new one.

The communist doctrine is one thing and communism is another. For the people, communism threatens to become a faith, not an individual but a common faith, a Church.   If this should unhappily occur, don't expect disappointments to deter them from their collective dream : nations do not make up their minds to try experiments quickly, but once started, they follow them to the bitter end, even to absurdity. You see, Mr. Roosevelt, the English and the Americans have always been islanders ; they have isolationism in their blood.   It is not easy for you to understand the need for unity of our European nations. You will point out, of course, that for centuries Europe has been the scene of fratricidal strife.   That is the whole point, the strife *is* fra-tricidal : horrible family quarrels, sometimes sordid, sometimes tragic, often absurd, like all family quarrels.   So much the worse for us, if you can only see territorial or economic rivalries.   You always talk as though we Nations had been born yesterday ; as though History had bequeathed us only stockbrokers' offices and other commercial establishments.   Certainly we have hated one another over boundary squabbles, like village joint heirs.   But we have also fought for very different reasons, doctrinal and sentimental ones, moral or religious ones.   We obviously cannot expect Hollywood's historical films to teach the American public that nationalism is a scourge of the modern world, that the Nation is an economic caricature of our old homelands, and that the thirteenth century was on the verge of bringing into existence, in spiritual Unity, the Federation of Homelands.   Which of you has the least idea of the nature of the authority of an international organisation like the University of Paris in those days, a thousand times more powerful, believe it if you can, than your League of Nations !

Dear Mr. Roosevelt, the lost opportunity was never found again— of course—for the simple reason that a century later the Economic question was already overshadowing the Social ; a ghastly preferment-selling Italy was building the foundations of capitalism and setting up the Dictatorship of Usury, control of which was to pass to Spain, until England wrenched it from her hands.   If America only wishes to have her turn, well and good ; we need go no further.   You have enough gold in your underground vaults, quilted with steel, to keep a bastard Society going for a couple of centuries ; it is neither Christian nor pagan, and like all creatures without ancestry or breeding, it possesses an enormous capacity for resistance, the vitality of a gutter-cat.   Nor will it die out, in the strict meaning of the term.   It will not decay, like the old pagan Society, which, like the seed in the earth, rotted only to sprout again.   Its technical perfection is quite likely to keep it going indefinitely, to keep it going at the cost of nations first, then of individuals, whose substance it will suck dry before itself becoming petrified.   In proportion as the causes of disorder double or triple, technical achievement will multiply tenfold, a hundred-fold its means of defence or repression.   Order will be maintained, but it will be like an orderly cemetery.   It will be maintained in the name of a Society of which only the administrative and police services will remain : a mere Skeleton. Human Society proper will no longer exist. Only there will be no one left to say so, for technical skill will have got the better of men's liberty and dignity long ago.

Dear Mr. Roosevelt, it is not just a matter of freeing Europe from Hitler. A cancer of which Hitler is merely one of the superficial symptoms must be torn up by the roots—or tomorrow even worse ones may occur. Chesterton wrote once that the world was full of Christian ideas gone mad. It is perhaps permissible to say even now that Fascism, Hitlerism, Communism shall one day appear, in the light of History, as monstrous deformations of the ancient idea of Christendom. Millions of men believe that they are finding in totalitarianism a Faith and a Religion with a spiritual element, morality and dogmas ; in the Party organisation, a Church ; in the all-knowing and all-powerful Dictator, a Pope or even a God. It would be disastrous to think you could set all these millions of men back on the right road by urging them no longer to worry about the fate of humanity, but to stick to their own little businesses ; even if you were to add the promise of shares at a moderate rate of interest. Let us call a spade a spade. There is no real unity between nations, there is none between individuals, without a common ideal ; and this ideal must be put at the highest possible level so that it may be seen from afar. Put it too low to make it more accessible, and the best are debased, the mediocre confirmed in their mediocrity. An exalted ideal need not be understood by every citizen individually ; it is enough that it is in the air, acting directly or indirectly, on men's consciences. Each single Englishman could not claim to grasp all that the Empire means, and yet to a certain extent he is Empire-minded. If I may be allowed this rather bald comparison, a similar state of mind existed in the twelfth and thirteenth centuries with regard to Christianity. The democrats believed they were being very shrewd in talking practical good sense : " Be democrats like the rest of us ; Democracy may be the régime which wastes most money ; but what is that to you, when you have none ? On the other hand, it asks no more, practically, than to live and let live. To every one his own little undertaking, and long live the Republic ! Where we are, citizens, no one need worry." But so it is ; the people formed the habit of " worrying " long ago ; they always have " worried ". They need to worry and to worry together, because solitude for one reason or another is a kind of luxury, the privilege of a certain number of abnormal idlers or chosen geniuses. One poor man's small undertaking is, moreover, never profitable enough to give him a high opinion of himself. This is doubtless why poor people like to pool their hopes, that is, their soul, so that there may be a little bit more for everyone.

Dear Mr. Roosevelt, when the democracies have won the war, the people of Europe will not think the job is over. Your people may, ours will not . . .   The people of Europe will not forgive the democracies for coming so late to their defence, or for not defending them at all. When this war is over, it will be the people who will have defended and saved the democracies.   For as long as possible, their democracies committed them to the very illusions to which a large part of American opinion adheres to-day.   The democracies made Munich : the people are in the process of making victory.   A victorious Europe will not be easy to lead.   Don't for an instant suppose that it will be enough to invite her to rest her weary bones, while the democracies get busy once more over her fate.   It is inconceivable that a world which, twice in twenty years, reached the brink of ultimate catastrophe should be told : " We give you the right to work out your own welfare ; what more do you want ? " when we know perfectly well that in a Society under the thraldom of money, freedom is a snare and a delusion.   It is in the nature of the old democracies to become more and more conducive to a coalition of financial interests, and of political parties linked to such interests, unless disrupted by the violence of parties representing the penniless.

Dear Mr. Roosevelt, this war will have thrown power-politics into disrepute, but it will not have raised politics in men's esteem.   The people will have lost still more illusions ; they will not have gained a faith.   History will say that the drama we are witnessing was one of great men and great peoples confronting each other—men of prey, of too debased a nature to be anything but men of prey, geniuses of destruction who continued to destroy even when they thought they were being constructive ; and on the other hand, great men who could, had they chosen so, have been men of prey too, their equals in strength and bearing, but who gave both to the cause of freedom, like Mr. Churchill and yourself.   Is that all ?   No.   For out of the chaos of contradictory events, one fact emerges.   Be it for Evil or for Good, everything that has been done has been done by the Leaders and by the People, against the Will of Money, against the Powers of Money which were whipped by their masters back into their golden cage.   It is Plutocracy which should come out beaten from this immense struggle. It was born in Europe, it has its roots in Europe and this is the one chance to cut at them.   Once the roots are cut, the repulsive vegetation which now covers the whole surface of the globe will soon wither and rot away.

Dear Mr. Roosevelt, Europe is ready, and you can count on my country.   Europe was not suffering from a crisis of low spirits, but from a crisis of anguish, and such neuroses, as you know, are usually the result of what psychiatrists call repression.   Our civilisation went on subsisting, but as though walled up in a system which allowed it no means of self-expression.   Europe is worth much more, and is a thousand times more precious, than the sort of civilisation (called rightly or wrongly capitalist) into which it fell almost by chance, for this civilisation is only a makeshift and a compromise. The machine-age developed so fast, with such lightening speed, that a provisional solution had hastily to be concocted for the new problem. You notice that I do not say another solution is impossible : I say it remains to be found, and that it goes against the grain for Europe to submit to the more or less hypocritical dictatorship of Money. The fine old peoples of Europe deserve something else ; they will not, for instance, put up indefinitely with the indiscriminate use of the word Property—honour being paid to both kinds without distinction—to describe the rights of a family of decent people to the land they have worked and improved for generations, for the general good, and those of any stockbroker to the fruits of his stockbroking.

To those people who would like to catch me out by asking me sardonically what I propose to do about it, I shall reply that I don't fancy myself as a reformer. I try to speak as clearly as I can in the name of millions of people who have no way of making themselves heard. We describe our pain, where it is, what it feels like, and then it is obviously the doctor's job to cure us. But if later on we find that he is again in league with the surgeon and the chemist to ruin us with equally ineffective operations and medicines, we'll wring his neck for him. Then at least we shall not die alone.

You see, Mr. Roosevelt, so many things have been done in your country with money, and have been done so quickly, that money still retains some of its prestige. It has allowed you to go full steam ahead, and to-day—for a little while, for the last time—it is enabling you to save the lives of men. But we no longer give it either respect or even awe ; it remains as arrogant and savage as ever, but it has become ridiculous. We used to accuse it of war-mongering. If that is what it is engaged on, it falls a victim to it, too. The profits it makes are clearly not proportionate to the increasing risks it runs. It is like some idiot who would set a whole town on fire in the hope of promoting his trade in fire-extinguishers. The men of money sought to increase their potency by cloaking themselves in the Principle of Property, like the lover in *Salambô* putting on Tanit's cloak. The Right of Property, through their ministrations, little by little assumed an absolute value, a sacred, almost magical character—but all in vain. By putting it beyond reach and discussion, they hoped they would themselves be out of reach. Unfortunately, all they did was to compromise the very Principle of Property itself.

Minds are in such a state of disorder that this talk of money and the men of money is liable to bring on my head the accusation that I am attacking the Principle, whereas in fact I am defending it. As well say that by condemning the traffic in Indulgences and the sale of Sacraments, the Council of Trent offended God ! It is absurd to go on giving the people the scandal of seeing speculators' profits guaranteed in the name of the commandment which forbids us to steal our neigh-bour's goods. Far from rejoicing that the Right to Property has fallen

on evil days, I deplore it. Political and economic nationalism has
undermined the idea of the Homeland ; Racism, the idea of Race ; the
dictatorship of Might, the principle of authority : religion itself emerges
weakened from all this equivocation . . . What can you offer the
people for their veneration ? What in the world are you going to give
them to love ?

The worst mistake of all would be precisely this—to abandon
Property to its fate. The people are so harrassed with all these
cynical inconsistencies, that they are now ready to hate it, calling it
Capital ; and all they will succeed in doing is to sink from the Capitalism
of the capitalists into State Capitalism. Angry and desperate, hungry
for change at any cost, they will let themselves be cemented within
this block of concrete. With the instinct of Property, they will lose
the instinct of Freedom. Is that what we are aiming at ? I realise
that the lie is so ubiquitous that no truth can be promulgated without
grave danger. What can I do about it ? When a man shores up a
damaged house, he runs the risk of having the roof come down on him.
Is that a reason for leaving the house to crumble to ruin, or not ? The
most imprudent thing would be to poke a little to right and left, here
repair a section of the wall, and there readjust the position of a beam.
The job must be tackled as a whole ; we must get the people of Europe
going in one great enterprise ; a total one, and one worthy of them too—
or else let Bolshevism do it in our stead, as I have already had the
honour of telling you. If the first goal to be aimed at can be made
quite clear, the hope aroused in men's hearts must be proportionate
to their present despair. I know it is fashionable among the bourgeoisie, and even among Christians—who could believe it !—to laugh
at whoever promises the moon. It is odd to hear such sneers issuing
from the lips of certain priests, sacriligeous lips which, every Christmas
day, have to repeat a promise—a thousand times more daring than the
promise of the moon—of Peace to all men of good will. We shall not
be content with promising the moon, we shall promise justice.

We shall promise justice and we shall begin by reinstating it where
injustice is now most rampant. What revolts the nations in our
social system is not—as they are supposed to say and as they may even
believe—the material power of Money, but rather that Money appears
not as a tyrant, but as a Master, a legitimate Master, honoured and
consecrated. What so bitterly wounds their conscience is, not seeing
the cowardly tremble before it, but the true Masters—those ancient
masters fallen from high estate—grown servile, but still quite recognis-
able, whose shame they cannot help sharing. It is, in short, seeing
Money, on the final lap of its cunning, cynical usurpations, gradually
asserting itself as a Moral and Spiritual power.

After all, Mr. Roosevelt, I am not a fool ; I quite understand that
human society will always be unjust to some extent ; but I have had
more than enough of the sneers meted out to the poor devils whom this
scandal hurts. It is the perpetual failures of human society which are

laughable, not the poor wretch who is so taken aback at seeing it every time, after a few awkward steps, always tumbling into the same hole. I can face the sneerers. They scornfully ask the poor fellow whether he wants justice everywhere and for everyone. And when he quietly says, Yes, like the catechism, they shrug their shoulders and turn away. But wait a moment, you fools ! The poor wretch was speaking his own language, and now I am going to speak in mine. We don't ask for absolute justice, but that injustice should be organised in a sufficiently human way, so that though inevitably crushing to flesh and blood, it is not intolerable to men's conscience. We don't ask for equality, but that inequalities be organised in such a way that, in their mutual rivalry, they cancel each other out as much as possible. To claim to have freed the people because only one privilege has been left standing, Money, the most humiliating of all, is one tremendous swindle. This sole privilege has added the weight of all the others to its own, and as it has no rivals, it prospers and waxes fat beyond all measure.

You see, Mr. Roosevelt, our old European societies, however out-of-date they may seem to-day, had achieved one very important thing. They had separated Prestige from Profit. So it is not true that they are inseparable. Where was almost all the gold of Europe in the thirteenth century ? In the hands of the Jews. When powerful monarchies needed gold, they had to borrow it from the Jews. Yet no one would maintain that the Jews were then shown signal honours ! " What does it matter ", you will say. Listen : it is not at all a bad thing not to have to pay reverence to the usurer who has got your pennies ; it's a sight for all the world to see. " Yet the poor wretches who chased after the Jewish millionaires, pelting them with rotten vegetables, had to bow low before the Lords of the Realm . . . " No, Sir. Each before *his* Lord, maybe, but not always his neighbour's, for the characteristic of a lord is precisely to stand by his own, as an act of pride if not of virtue. A point of honour if you like. Moreover, the nobleman's prestige was offset by the priest's and the Magistrate's had to be taken into account, and that of countless institutions, corporations, confraternities and communities, each with its own status. A proverb of my country says that when the cats fight, the mice dance. The rivalry between the various prestiges and privileges, their inextricable interlacings, their constantly renewing conflicts, which our Monarchy almost always solved to the advantage of the people, in accordance with popular feeling, did after all leave the poor folk room to breathe . . . These prestiges and privileges had one arbiter, the King. And for exactly this reason they could have no solidarity : they were rivals. The solidarity of the economic privileges, despite appearances, is as unrelenting as Hell.

Democratic American bourgeois need not think I long to see the *ancien régime* of my country imposed on them. It has been made quite ridiculous enough, in your idiotic films, for me to take my modest revenge by telling them frankly that I do not consider they have yet

become the sort of men who would be likely to find themselves at home
in a revival of any of our great epochs ; they would feel a bit cramped.
No, Mr. Roosevelt, I want neither for you nor for France herself a
restoration of the past which would be as artificial as historical wax-
works. This is what I mean : in any society, under any régime
whatever, the moment the absurd dictatorship of profit is smashed,
out of the nature of things and the experience of men will grow some
sort of system based upon the same principles.

I am so tired of hearing the democracies opposed to the dictatorships,
even by M. Maritain. The simple truth is that Democracy is defence-
less against dictators. Any democracy can throw a dictatorship-crisis
overnight, like appendicitis ; and national idiosyncrasy is no help.
No nation is more different from the German nation than the Italian ;
yet, if the former were wolf-born, it did not cost the latter much to turn
into a hyena or jackal. And at this point in the argument, I have had
enough of being told that by rejecting the democrats I am playing up
to the totalitarians. If my only choice is between these two creations
of the modern world, that is its fault, and not mine. There is no
American living more devoted to the Bill of Rights than I am, or who
better understands its meaning, for the reason that it was men like
myself who formulated it.   But democracy is no more the Bill of Rights
than General Franco's clerical dictatorship is the Gospel. Democracy
is the political form of Capitalism, in the same sense that the soul is
the Form of the body, in Aristotle's sense, or its Idea, according to
Spinoza. Capitalism, as it emerged, established itself and grew,
gradually transformed democracy to its own needs. No power on
earth will stop it from pursuing its destiny. It is useless to tell me
that tomorrow's Democracy will not be like the old ones. If it's a
matter of changing names, what am I to say. Montesquieu wrote
that the mainspring of Monarchies is honour, that of Democracies,
virtue. I wonder if poor devils are really incited to virtue by being
given the right to vote and no bread : their vote is then the only thing
they can sell for bread.
    Everybody talks about restoring spiritual values ; it is a fashionable
phrase. Spiritual values will never be restored, so long as profit is
honoured when it should only be tolerated and controlled. A society
which turns any publican grown well-to-do through the sale of poison
to the hungry into a person of consequence, a bourgeois—people who
in Caracalla's day were called *honestiores*—and makes outcasts of the
destitute wretches he poisons, is a society standing on its head. Even
should we like to defend it, really we could not go crusading with a
society with such distressing habits. We remember that the Roman
Empire died for having made a similar attempt to defy the natural
equilibrium of human posture. It is indeed a great mistake to believe
that the Roman Empire washed its hands of Social Justice. Unfortunately, as in the modern democracies, it was a matter that concerned

only governmental departments and civil servants. In the second century, the corporations were privileged, and agencies to feed the populace multiplied : *pueri mammaeani, puellae mammaeanae.* It lent money to the poor, interest free, to allow them to buy land ; it handed out scholarships to the children of the poor. The Illyrian Emperors legislated copiously for the benefit of widows and orphans, and a little later, under the Valentinian dynasty, the State never perhaps had a more clear idea of its social duty—to what avail !

In the clash between laws and customs, customs always win, and customs, then as now, favoured Profit. Overshadowed by the colossal imperial administration, with its meddling and crushing solicitude, budding Christianity had nothing to give except hope. And what hope ? Certainly not that of a proletarian dictatorship ! But that of a society where the poor would be honoured, because God himself had taken on poverty and beatified it : not only as certain simoniacal theologians sometimes let it be understood, the moral disposition of poverty of spirit, but the social condition of being poor. The Empire poured out laws, bureaucrats and gold all in vain. As between Christianity and the Empire, the disinherited masses put their trust in Christianity, for so honour was restored to them.

It doesn't matter to me if this point of view strikes the realists as comic. Had I been born in the second century, they would not only have laughed heartily, they would have thrown me to the lions, which seems to me no more cruel than to be scattered to the winds by a two-thousand pound bomb. The part played by honour, and the profits that accrued to Society on its account, are not so negligible as these gentlemen think. Is it not a prodigious achievement of honour, always, for instance, to have found soldiers at its beck and call—that is, as a rule, underpaid and under-nourished men whose glory comes from dying in defence of the goods of the well-to-do, and who consider themselves handsomely rewarded by a bugle-blast over their graves, or a twenty-five franc Cross ?

So the undermining of the prestige of Money is no small undertaking. If I were an anarchist, I should not take so much upon myself. But then I am not an anarchist. A frontal attack on Profit involves the double risk of endangering real values and, at the same time, necessary evils which are a species of value. For a blind revolt against Money threatens the downfall of the civilisation in which it is so intricately involved, and men of money are not unaware of this. They hope to trap us in a hopeless dilemma : whether to preserve institutions which they have every intention of corrupting, as they have always done, or to suffer dictatorship as the only means of reducing them to impotence. " You'll get the better of us only at the price of your own freedom", they tell us. But the men of money forget just one thing : that a tyranny is done for the day it ceases to be respected—that is, as soon as its downfall is conceivable. Spiritual Forces will do away with the Tyranny of Money, because they will free men's conscience and will make men's conscience stand up to these and any other masters. And then the united front of Freedom will be a reality.

Have you noticed what an immense amount of talk there is about spiritual forces, of a kind which seems to imply that your famous Relief legislation intends to have them produced by Henry Ford ? Obviously we shall never know the mysterious laws which govern the birth and ceaseless development of spiritual forces. A sea captain in former times knew just as little of the physics of the origin of winds, tides and ocean currents, yet he used them with no less skill, because of his sea-sense. A sense of spiritual things is still unfortunately much more rare than sea-sense. If we had it, we would always find, almost unerringly, the necessary spiritual forces, and human beings to embody them. A straightforward consideration of the great movements of History shows them up as groundswells, and the men of genius who appear upon the surface as drawn up from the depths and hurled like arrows to the foamy crests, whence they seem to rule the sea . . .

The storm is gathering over Europe, and I am not thinking of the present war. It is easy to mistake the crash of collapse for the roar of thunder. The present war is a collapse. If I may compare the dim forebodings of many souls to a purely material phenomenon, I should say that the storm I have in mind is still only at the stage of that shuddering of the air which precedes all great wind and sea disturbances. Please do not listen to the economists who, with economists' arguments, are probably trying to persuade you that Europe is at the end of its tether. I would rather you saw Europe at an end of illusions and lies, so placed that a mere shift in equilibrium can tip it into Evil or into Good. So it is : either those spiritual forces, whose rumblings make her anxious and stir her foundations, will combine, or else the opportunity will be lost, the miracle a dud ; they will crash in a turmoil of which the honourable Members of Congress in Washington may unfortunately have only a very sketchy notion. Economists suppose that hungry nations are incapable of ardent longing, or of getting down to a job. Nothing could be further from the truth. It is replete nations that sleep supine and dream no dreams.

Europe's present system is not very different from that of the eleventh century. Oh, how I wish that my well-meaning readers would see in such a parallel more than a debating point ! We are hardly forty years from the happy days when the invention of the balloon, motor-car and aeroplane announced the abolition of war, and vaccines and serums, the suppression of disease . . . We were so pleased with ourselves, so naïvely sure of being one up on the Past ; we should have been so proud of showing Rameses II, Alexander the Great, Caesar, Mahomet, Charles V and Louis XIV round the *Exposition Universelle* of 1900, like country cousins. Indeed, when you come to think of it, we are to-day much closer to a man of the year One Thousand than we are to a contemporary of Napoleon III. Our distress is like his, because it is just as undefined. Like him, we ask, where are we going ? For like him we feel we shall not find what we have lost, or we shall find it in a new form and unrecognisable—we feel that we are witnessing the end of a world, without knowing anything sure of the one which will replace it, if indeed it is to be replaced at all !

The people of the year One Thousand were the survivors of a double collapse, of the Empire of the Caesars and of the Empire of Charlemagne. They were decimated by war and pestilence, grounds for their condemnation according to the preachers of the day. As gold was scarce, the well-to-do were more overbearing than ever, the Jews more avaricious, the few traders more thieving, those in power more grasping, the destitute more poverty-stricken. Yes, the world must have seemed to everyone even more decrepit than it seems to-day. A Frenchman of 1940 is separated only by two or three centuries from an era of refined humanism and extraordinarily attractive ways of life. What an abyss of time stretched between a man of the year One Thousand and the splendours of the Roman Order ! . . . Well, Mr. Roosevelt, in that aged, worn-out world, of which the Wise despaired and which the Monks described as sold to the Devil— Chivalry was invented. Please don't expect me to indulge in ecstasies over that institution ; once it is printed, this book may fall into any hands. As the years go by, I find there are very few things I cannot talk about to all and sundry, but I really haven't the courage to explain what Chivalry was, to some of your opponents, for example, whom you see at much closer quarters than I do, Mr. Roosevelt ; I know the expression on their faces . . . I only want to say, Chivalry was not born of a fit of optimism ; it flowered upon the selfishness, savagery and despair of the world. So tomorrow, perhaps . . .

Dear Mr. Roosevelt, this lovely miracle, this miracle of the spirit of heroism and the spirit of childhood—this childlike miracle—is perhaps not so far from us. I say this, because it is still very absurd to say it—so absurd that it is a secret one can tell without giving it away ; no passer-by will recognise it in its fool's motley, and the fool will slip quietly between the tables at Belshazzar's feast, through the mummers and the lutenists, to write his message on the wall . . . You see, the collapse of institutions, even of respectable institutions, should not affect us, for the time is past when institutions could still save men. There are times when men are only conscious of danger through régimes and systems ; régimes and systems are what they defend or restore. Don't you agree, however, that such times are already gone ? People are baffled, they feel themselves let down, not merely by what they served, for love or gain, but personally, in their deep personal feeling for truth or falsehood, justice and injustice. If they still want to believe in something, they must believe in themselves, they must come to terms with their own souls again. Such a state of affairs has seldom been seen in the course of History, but each time the best men have come forward and met mysteriously in a secret, unexpected tryst. And deserted systems and régimes were suddenly found empty, and long-forgotten places thronged with vast crowds.

Those who assert that Europe will not be able to extricate herself from chaos unaided are not wrong, if they mean by Europe the parties and organised factions of Europe. But they are abominably wrong if they believe that the men of Europe, those worthy of the name of man, the free men, will let themselves die like rats in the rubble, when the roof over their heads comes down on them. One by one they will crawl out on all fours, wriggling through the tiniest gaps ; they will dig out stones, and scratch at the earth with their fingernails. I hope I may be allowed these figures of speech. They are one way of setting out a concrete fact which could equally well be explained in very different language. The men of Europe have been taken in by calls to order and ideologies inspiring mutual hatred. It is absolutely impossible for you Americans to understand how cruel these experiences have been, because the occasional news of them that reaches you is naturally brought over by intellectuals ; and those who suffered worst are precisely the ones who went through this inner crisis of the soul with no means to intellectualise it. Pay no attention to what the petty teachers of the pre-war generation may have said about it, in their so-called Youth papers. The calls to order and ideologies they used merely to cover themselves, as alibi or means of self-justification. But the men I mean claimed justification for man and for life. And they were let down. They see now, or will see tomorrow, that all that was great, disinterested and true in them was their own greatness, disinterestedness and faith. God grant that tomorrow they recognise one another, like the men who, nearly a thousand years ago, out of disgust with all sham orders, got together and invented a new Order : the order of honour. Not the honour of a party, or a system, or even of a country, but the honour of Man and, if I may repeat what I have written in another book, the honour of Honour.

Your Hollywood historians seem to think that mediaeval chivalry was recruited among the Powerful first. Nothing could be further from the truth. It was the powerful men who sought it, once the title of knight had become more dazzling than any other. They ruined the institution ; indeed they ruined it very quickly—in a century or two at most—but by then it was impossible for anyone to suppress its spirit. Why ? For a very simple reason : the Church had consecrated it. We shall never know whether the opulent Roman prelates were or were not acting from political motives. But supposing they were : God is using the Church, even when the opulent prelates cherish the illusion they are using Him. By whatever door it comes in, what the Church has once consecrated can no longer leave it, can never, never leave it, for now not political prelates but millions of pure and simple souls are handing it safely down the centuries : do you see ? Chivalric honour, which means reversing the world's values, scorning money, exalting poverty, reverencing strength only for coming to the help of the weak—strength confined to service—all this was, once for all, consecrated by the Church. It became the Christian prototype of honour, the orthodox prototype of honour. Out of prudence or self-interest, Churchmen, Princes among the Priests or Scribes, may mention it as seldom as possible, choosing some other topic of conversation with the Rich and Powerful; honour is nonetheless there, in reserve, guaranteed by the witness of the Saints, as is your dollar by the counter-signature of the Secretary of the Treasury and the Treasurer of the United States. Please don't imagine I am trying to convert anyone to Papistry. But you see, I have nothing to my name but this tradition of my race and country; I shall leave my children nothing else. And I am happy that its title-deeds were entrusted to an ancient and illustrious Institution which, through two thousand years, saddled with more or less able and sometimes dishonest administrators, has never, in fact, gone back on its word.

Of course, I have no idea what this new incarnation of Christian Honour, meaning the hereditary Honour of the men of Europe, will be like. I know that the elements that will compose it are ready, that is all; they are " in presence," as the scientists say, and if they do not succeed in combining, there goes the world's last chance. When I speak of restoring Christian honour, I do not mean a religious revival in the literal sense. It is doubtful whether after the peoples' appalling frustration, they will come straight back to the faith. Those who no longer hope for justice in this world are not so near hoping for it in the next as a certain number of pious men and women think, as though a man turns to God for lack of something better. What I mean is a revolt of Christian honour. Christian honour can revolt among believers or unbelievers equally easily, for it is the underlying principle in both types of conscience and was handed down to both.

To use the term chivalry in connection with this revolt may seem to be flying in the face of good sense. No, but it is flying in the face of the fools' way of thinking. So now I have made them a present of something to joke about, a final laugh before the men I herald wring their necks. You realise of course I am not proposing a return to ancient ritual, with armed vigil, coats of mail and spurs of gold : I am no archivist or antiquarian. I use the word *knight* because it jars on realistic ears. But once the day has come—if ever I see that day !— I shall find another. When the steps of brave men ring on the land, my land, if I am underneath, still I shall hear them. I say to the imposters of all régimes and systems and parties ; to the masters of Usury as well as of Force ; to the servile intellectuals, the simoniacal doctrinaires : " Here, here, come the men to whom you lied ! "

Perhaps this is only a dream. Frustrated men easily turn into anarchists. They may devour one another. They may try that supreme form of totalitarianism, the dictatorship of the proletariat ; supposing it to be their own and not realising that in any dictatorship whatever the last word always goes to the bureaucrats and police.

Nonetheless, the fact to which I have drawn your attention remains.
The present war is quite different in character from those which
preceded it ; how much do you know this, in America ?   Millions of
men have made themselves outlaws ; I mean, outlaws of a society for
which they had no more use, or in which they had ceased to believe.
(There is a difference.) The former would have none of it and set
about destroying it ; the latter had lost faith in it and did nothing
to defend it.   Don't assume they were all despicable men.   Before
they were converted, the Christian martyrs of the first centuries would
not have died either for the gods whom they honoured or pretended to
honour from sheer force of habit.   I shall call the men I was speaking
of the Unemployed, if you don't mind, Mr. Roosevelt.   They no longer
know—or soon will not know—how to occupy either their hands or
their hearts.   Forgive this romantic metaphor.   The economists of
your Economic Bureau will retort that unemployment of the heart is
no business of theirs, but that there will be plenty of jobs for hands,
in Reconstruction alone.   The economists of your Economic Bureau
amuse me.   Long before Reconstruction begins, speculation on reconstruction will have started, and one will be swallowed by the other,
like the male by the female praying mantis.   Ah, well, to some forms
of frustration and bitterness of heart, not even manual labour can
bring ease or forgetting.   Once again, the demilitarisation of the
dictatorships will not settle everything.   Take, for instance, a young
French bourgeois and a young French workman who, puzzled by
infamous propaganda, faltered at the crucial moment between duty to
class and duty to nation, but aware now of having betrayed class
and nation ; they will not be easier subjects for readaptation than the
demobilised troops of the Dictatorships.   This question of unemployment takes many different forms in the different categories of
unemployed.   The sale of Oregon apples was a great help to yours.
But we really cannot suggest to these men that they sell apples.

Mr. Roosevelt, on reading certain pages of this book, many of your
compatriots will certainly take me for anti-democratic.   At least,
this is the accusation I expect from a number of American Catholics,
who used to uphold the " good dictators", Mussolini and Franco,
against M. Maritain and myself.   I believe, however, that I have always
been a free man.   My fondness for freedom is not merely platonic and
sentimental.   It is not enough for me to have freedom proclaimed by
law : I should want to know how the law proposes to defend it.   This
is where Americans could pay heed to the time-old experience of the
people of Europe.   Under the protection of liberal laws framed for
free men and for their use, mediocre men only sink a little lower each
day into the spirit and habits of servitude.   Thus, the freedom of the
press is a great thing ; but if citizens take advantage of the fact that
this freedom is guaranteed by their Constitution to give up thinking
altogether, that is, if they allow it to justify their inclination to

conform and support in turn just those opinions which favour their own concerns; then freedom of thought will soon be a mere slogan to be exploited by imposters on political platforms.   I am not anti-democratic.   On the contrary, I deplore that this word democrat, which used to stand for a man of deep conviction, vision and faith, should have sunk to mean merely a citizen in a democracy, so that we may witness, any day now (though not for long), democracies without democrats, free régimes without free men.

How absurd this game of prophets can become ; but my prophecy is surprising and shocking, even more than absurd : out of Europe's disaster, out of the collapse of the dictatorships, out of our frustration and misery, there may arise, tomorrow, a generation of free men : truly free, not just honestly disposed to enjoy the advantages of freedom up to the very gates of slavery.   These will be men who suffered greatly in mind and body.   I say they *may* arise, only so as not to frighten you.   At heart, I am already sure they will come ; it is for them I am writing.   Laugh at me, exclaim what a fine paradox it is to expect you to look forward to lessons in freedom from fellows who are now tampering with the freedom of others or powerless to defend their own.   You need feel no concern, however : they'll not want to give you lessons in freedom, for the very good reason that harsh, cruel, terrible experience will have proved to them that no one can be taught freedom, or receive it as a gift even : its strength is inside a man, a power of the soul.   A free nation is one which includes a certain proportion of proud men, and if the proper proportion is not reached, there is no point in getting the lawyers to declare it free.   You see how necessary it is to be sure of the meaning of words.   I shall go on saying again and again that there are in America, as elsewhere, men who claim to be lovers of freedom simply because they are in a position to enjoy it.   Far from being ready to make sacrifices for it, they take for granted that it is there to relieve them of sacrifices and let them prosper in peace, or even to contribute to their prosperity.   In these cases, the statement " I am a free man " means, " My country's political constitution gives me the right to concentrate on my cupidity : and if a certain amount of disinterestedness, or even heroism, is in fact indispensable in every society, even a realistic one, I will pay for someone else to be heroic or disinterested for me."

Perhaps Providence will not entrust the fate of freedom tomorrow only to the democrats of the Democracies.   The democrats of the Democracies have made a great habit of freedom, but we know for a fact that habit kills love.   Had the democrats of the democracies really loved freedom, we should not have seen them, for instance, shamefully glorying in Munich.   It was not freedom they went to seek at Munich, but peace, peace at any price.   In their hearts, they prefer peace to freedom, or rather they confuse the two.   Is " peace " really the word to use ?   Would they not even confuse selfishness with freedom?

If you Americans want men really devoted with all their might to freedom, they must not be mediocrities. Mediocre men who have lived a long time in an atmosphere of freedom will of course protest most lustily on hearing that they are suddenly to be deprived of an environment to which they are accustomed ; but their struggles are most unlikely to last much longer than the time needed to make the operation effective, that is, to transfer them from the aquarium labelled " *democracy* " to the aquarium labelled " *dictatorship*."

I want you Americans to realise how much the men of Europe have suffered ; and this will give them an enormous advantage over you. Granted, from a distance they may look like madmen, savages, idiots. Yet they are neither idiots nor savages ; they know the worth of what they shattered in their wrath or let others shatter in their despair. The dull resignation of some, the blind violence of others, have the same meaning—a refusal. To use a colloquial expression, almost slang, these people were fed up ; when a horse is fed up, he lies down in his tracks, or kicks over the traces. Have you never felt like doing that yourselves ? You found in fact that post-war society filled you with enthusiasm and love ? Well, so much the better for you ; that is all I can say. But do in all fair-mindedness look at it from another point of view, if only for a brief moment : something has obviously been happening in Europe during the last thirty years, for certain nations to go mad and others to become stricken, prostrate, numb. You will say that there is no explanation for these unhappy occurrences ; the Old Continent had everything a continent needs, old or young : banks, factories, shops—plenty of shops, for the day-time, and music-halls to while away the nights. True, true enough . . . But, you see, we lacked heart to fill our days or while away our nights. The men of Europe were stifling, they longed for a breath of air. " What ! " you will say. " Are we to believe that they rushed into slavery, or allowed themselves to be dragged into it, for love of freedom ? " Not for love, dear friends, but out of disgust. It's all very fine to put freedom, like love, within the reach of everyone, but the thing is to know, *what* freedom and *what* love. After a little reflection we see that the democracies were dispensing freedom just as certain houses dispense love : " Pay me heavy taxes, citizens, ever-increasing taxes. At such a price you will be free, without being put to any trouble, and even almost without being aware of it." On these terms freedom is merely comfort, whereas it should be the most magnificent of risks, the ultimate risk. We had let the notion of freedom fall so low that in the end Lenin's terrible sneer, his appalling cynicism was on the lips of men everywhere : " Freedom ? For what ? " You can protest that his blasphemy is absurd. All blasphemies are absurd, but a man blasphemes only when he has loved, only where he has believed.

The men of Europe will have suffered enough by tomorrow for the word freedom to have a new meaning for most of them, or at least a renewed meaning—the meaning it has for a prisoner in his cell, for a humiliated man in his shame.   I am thinking not only of the men who were led to believe that freedom is a mere legal abstraction, a fiction not worth dying for—in which, after all, they differed very little from the democrats, the Munich democrats—and who believed they would rediscover greatness in the depth of utter slavery, therefore pledging to a leader, a party, that inalienable portion of themselves without which obedience is only servitude and forgetfulness of self a betrayal. I am thinking of others too, even of you Englishmen, surprised by threatening death in the middle of an academic discussion on communism, anti-communism and the rights of conscientious objectors, and roused at last by the outrage to the name and honour of England.

Men of Europe, what will remain of your appalling experience, except the bitter certainty that you were more or less taken in ? Those who believed they could entrust the safeguarding of their freedom to institutions saved themselves from slavery only by means of cold steel.   And those who trusted to cold steel are now themselves threatened with slavery.   Men of Europe, Men of Europe ! there is no true salvation left but in yourselves.   Before racking your brains to choose among the political and social systems which the lawyers will lay before you, remember this : legislation cannot go on indefinitely bolstering up weaknesses of heart and spirit, and the law protects the weak effectively only if it is itself protected against simony and corruption by proud men strong in the tradition of unwritten law and justice according to the Spirit.   You will see that all freedom, like all pride, hangs together, and the humiliation of the weak is a direct blow at the honour and prestige of the strong, debasing and degrading the very idea of strength ; but in the name of justice you will refuse to pay homage to that idol of all conformist Societies— legality as a substitute for Right.

When we say democracy, Mr. Roosevelt, we may not be thinking of the same thing.   Never mind.   It will not be wholly untrue one day to say that the gold, power and labour of American democracy saved England.   It will be truer still to declare that England's heroic example had first saved American democracy from itself, ready as it was for a colossal Munich.   I don't mind fairly loose talk about English democracy, but in the name of this same tolerance, may I point to a much more complex historic reality—the English Monarchy and English Tradition, which made the Englishman long before the word democracy had come into general use : the English Man, to whom your people owes so much.

We may not agree on the precise meaning of democracy, but we certainly think the same thing about a great number of democrats. If you entrust such people with democracy, they won't hesitate to sacrifice it to their peace and comfort at the first opportunity, and with no remorse, for they sincerely feel that a democracy which requires sacrifices, that is, one where a man cannot go on lining his pockets in safety, ceases then and there to be a democracy. You have had to defend American democracy against such fools, and totalitarian propaganda simulated horror at what it called your abuse of power. But the danger does not lie in the abuse of power, but in the democrats' secret liking for the arbitrary. Dreading above all else having to make an effort, they much prefer the State to make the effort for them, and as the exercise of universal suffrage gives them the illusion of being able to say, with Louis XIV, " *L'Etat c'est nous !* " they pretend that nothing is lost, while in fact everything has been handed over to the anonymous monster. The democratic masses never took on this war like men ; they let themselves be dragged into it by the provocations and brutalities of the dictators ; they went into it shying away from it, driven by the will of a small number of free men, proud men, whom we shall doubtless see them disclaim tomorrow, just as yesterday our French democracy disclaimed Georges Clémenceau. When victory is won, I am much afraid they will immerse themselves in State collectivism, surging to it like cattle to a stable with lowings of contentment. And this is clearly no joke. You know better than I, for instance, what the instruments and beneficiaries of Mr. Chamberlain's policy are saying to one another in England, and the intellectuals, who are even more despicable. What an outlook, with snobbery, selfishness and fear in eventual collusion !

I am afraid Anglo-Saxon conservatism has been taken too seriously. The Anglo-Saxons conserve more by habit than by choice, like a sick man hanging on to an old tooth ; and they even hang on to it so long that, from periostitis to asteitis, in the end they find it quite normal to have their molar removed by a surgeon and a bit of the jawbone too. When a conformist nation shifts from one conformity to another, you may be sure that it will not do it by halves . . . We are really sick of hearing individualism denounced as the cause of all our ills, for modern society has gone on for a hundred and fifty years, mass-producing types of men less and less distinguishable from each other. It is not enough to endow poor beggars with the name of citizen to raise them to the status of ancient Romans of Rome. For these citizens of modern democracies, the name administrees is far more suitable. It is no use to say it is better to be a mere administree than slave to Hitler. The answer is that one dictatorship leads to another, and tax-payers who are used to wait shivering in queues outside office doors, or to mop their brows in agony trying to decipher the mystifying edicts of a host of anonymous fuehrers, will one day or another make excellent cattle for totalitarian herds. Let me add this : sheer hatred for the hypocritical dictatorship of bureaucracy sometimes sets violent men dreaming of finding themselves a master, a real live one with blood, not ink, in his veins.

Letter to the Europeans

November, 1941.

MEN of Europe! Men of Europe! Let me be your witness, now that the rest of the world has ceased to believe in you. A man who was not in the Secret of your history and destiny could naturally not watch you tear one another to pieces without being revolted. I do try to understand you and I am not conscious of indulging in simplified *gobinisme* when I point out that, after all, there are only a few centuries between you and your forefathers, whom the Roman imperial bureaucrats called Barbarians—which meant that they were rebels, enemies of the law, more than savages. Barbarian sounded to Roman ears like revolutionary to many people to-day. And revolutionaries they were, without knowing it; they drew from their old military, amorous and roving stock a certain feeling for freedom which might easily appear anarchical to a Roman Procurator, for it was less a feeling than an instinct. Believe me, what was said in their poor hovels or on the village greens was much the same as you hear to-day in any public house. At the appropriate moment, they found it perfectly natural to break with the bourgeois—" Let's make a clean slate of the Past "—and they tried to find an original type of civilisation, one frankly founded on distrust of men of law, moneylenders, state officials and traders : just the four kinds of men from whom they suffered most during their enslavement. Fumblingly, they set up a very complicated system—but one which time would have simplified in the long run—of reciprocal obligations guaranteed by free contracts, so that obedience could truly be given the name of Loyalty. I do not deny that this venture miscarried. It failed because they were betrayed. For centuries, all our history has been a gradual, inexorable restoration of the Pagan Order on to a very rudimentary Christian civilisation in which the clerics themselves probably never had faith, they never had the heart to stake anything on it.

Men of Europe! Men of France! All these historical considerations are Greek to most of you, I know ; it is none the less true that the Order which has so long been imposed on you is not your order. It is not the one you would have made, nor the one you had begun to make. Forty years ago, all discussion on this point would have seemed purely speculative, for no one dared call this order by its true name. Now you know it for what it is ; you judge our civilisation by its works, the tree by its fruit. If you are not careful, relentless logic will tomorrow impose on it the restoration of slavery, or even—and why not ?—the deification of Fuehrers. Your temporal and spiritual masters lied when they asked you to believe that all they had done was to fuse present and past. They hid the monster from your sight as long as they could, they may even have retarded its development. Now look at it, full-grown, with its normal complement of claws and teeth ; it will be useless now to call this tiger a cat, or tickle it under the chin in the hope of making it purr. " The pagan State is revived ! " —there is the warning which should ring out night and day, if there are still men. The Pagan State is not only reincarnate in institutions ; it has stamped itself upon mind and conscience. Communists or totalitarians—workers or bourgeois—each conceives the god in a different form and prays to him according to the appropriate rites ; but all beg for his kingdom to come : *adveniat regnum tuum !* Nations no longer want to run risks or to live their lives as nations just as a man worthy of the name lives a man's life. To-day, as twenty centuries ago, they base their hopes on a colossal bureaucracy. Too cowardly to take on responsibilities of their own accord, and shivering in anticipation of the mess their vices will lead them into, they gladly hand over to the Administration the job of saving them from themselves and making them do what has to be done, so long as due deference is paid to their vanity, and they can go on calling themselves voters and be apparently in control of the enormous machine. They know that, at the rate things are going, the Government will be so powerful to-morrow, and its universal regimentation so detailed, that, with the vote becoming a purely honorific privilege, as empty as the title Canon of the Lateran conferred by the Pope on each successive President of the Republic, a change of deputies or senators will have no more importance than a change of umbrellas. What of it ! All they want is to make their system even more complicated. The London press itself gave out triumphantly the other day that Scientists must be incorporated, the salvation of the democracies demanding it. I ask you, what country esteemed scientists more highly than Germany ? Sterilising the abnormal, eliminating inferior products, applying to our species the ordinary procedures of Selection, and in everything concerning the weak following the example of nature, which, far from treating them kindly, sacrifices them ruthlessly to the strong—all that seems to me terrifically scientific. But let it pass. Committees of psychologists will argue with committees of moralists and committees of theologians until the citizens, last indefeasible right is warranted by half a score of government offices open daily from nine till five, excepting, of course, on Sundays and holidays.

What a programme of work for the formulators of Regulations ! But however complicated our administration is, it is child's play compared to that of the Roman Empire a few years before the accession of Constantine . . . The Pagan State has come back to life with a vengeance. But listen a moment : this does not mean that the leaders of the State will stop going to confession, you sillies. What it does mean is that an ever-growing number of men refuse the heroic part in life, refuse to wager, with Pascal, on eternal values. It is not that they all turn them down. But those who do still believe in them will not risk a wager, that is all ; they feel in no mood to stake their destinies on a chance. Even did they want to, they could not. They have lost the sense of justice ; they have become quite incapable of longing for justice with that longing which the Gospel blandly likens to hunger and thirst. All they ask is that they personally shall suffer as little as possible from injustice, and so they make themselves very small ; they shrink down to elude its grasp ; they studiously avoid having any distinguishing marks so as to be sure of losing themselves in the herd. When men set out to pool their mediocrity, the Pagan State is then conceived and it will not stop growing. Men will become more and more mediocre and the State will become more and more powerful. When they reach a certain level of perfection in mediocrity, uniformity and gregarious discipline, their dignity as men will be lost, and the State will be God. And the name under which we worship it is of no account—Democracy or Dictatorship.

Men of Europe, you have not suffered so much only to start all over again in an experiment which has been tried a hundred times and a hundred times come to nothing. It is not true, as Jean-Jacques Rousseau asserted, that man is born good and that Society corrupts him. Nor is it true that Society, endlessly perfectable, is endlessly capable of improving man's condition. The moment always comes when Society asks for more than it gives, and when the least increase in well-being means yielding an essential liberty. It is considered clever to make fun of people who seek the Kingdom of God in this world. But those who want to set up the Reign of Man are brewing themselves even more bitter disappointments, for the earthly paradise is no less inaccessible than the other, and if humankind were to succeed in finding the way again, it would reach it in an utterly degraded state : the earthly paradise has become the paradise of beasts.

Men of Europe, it is quite absurd for me to try to speak to you, but, after all, no more absurd than my messages to Mr. Roosevelt or Mr. Churchill, or to the dead in the last war, with whom, for twenty-three years, I have carried on a conversation which is one long monologue. Beware of the peace ! The last was a fine rat-trap, but this one will be on the scale of a pit to catch wild elephants ; and if you fall into it right away, you will never clamber out. Go down step by step, cling tightly to the slope, men of Europe ! And from the very start, be sure of this, all of you : a great number, a very great number of the men who will pride themselves on having freed you from the dictators were formerly—morally at least—their accomplices. Whatever survives of the horrid old greybeards or the cynical whipper-snappers to whom we owe the casuistry of Non-Intervention will shout : " Long live Freedom ! " louder than all the rest. You must refuse to take it from such hands. Only the other day, behind your backs at Munich, those same irresponsibles, uttering the name of Freedom, obviously could not look one another in the face without laughing. Suppose that, forty-eight hours before the 1940 Armistice, by some miraculous event, glanders, the itch or the plague had decimated the German Army ; that Pétain and Weygand had suddenly, in spite of themselves, turned out to be victorious : those two cronies would be talking to Frenchmen to-day in the same terms as others will tomorrow. Beware, beware, men of Europe ! If you are not careful, what the dictators wanted to do in a few years will be done in fifty or a hundred ; but the result will be the same ; the State will have conquered everything, drawn everything to itself, absorbed everything ; you will have escaped the totalitarian demi-gods merely to slip slowly down to the slime of the anonymous dictatorship. The State will have taken charge of your welfare for good and all, and death alone will free you from its overpowering solicitude.

Listen to me. They are trying to make you believe that there is no way of standing up to this monstrous growth, and that it is in the nature of things. But I tell you that it is not in the nature of men ; that man, if he want to, can have the last word. A favourite fallacy of the nitwits to-day makes out that their last shred of liberty is bound to be snatched away from them sooner or later, and so they resign themselves to it beforehand. But it will not be snatched away ; they themselves will let go of it, as of all the rest ; they will loosen their hold without even noticing it, and the lynx-eyed State will gather up the threads and add them to its collection. For the overweening power of the State is simply the measure of our own increasing slackness. The Temporal prospers on whatever is lost by the Spiritual. Will you never realise this ? The state is an insurance against risks. If you want to be guaranteed against legitimate, indispensable risks of the sort a man cannot reject without dishonour, then stop calling yourself Citizen and take the appropriate name of Pauper.

It is not true that there is nothing left to oppose to this colossal, nightmarish creation of the herd instinct, and that it has grown beyond the stage when it could still be considered vulnerable. There is no point in wanting to set up a rival institution, born of the same spirit ; there would be the risk of falling from one slavery into a worse, like the Germans, Russians, Italians or Spaniards. The State fears but one rival, man. Man alone, I mean man free. Not the brutal, summary intractables, not the intellectual anarchists who are the most absurd of all intellectuals, and to borrow Proudhon's famous expression, the most " femmelin ". I say the free man, not the dialectician or the brute ; a man capable of scrupulous self-discipline, but never accepting it blindly from outside. A man to whom the supreme in " comfort " is the possibility of doing what he likes when he likes, at least to some extent, even though the cost of this choice he so highly values is loneliness and poverty ; a man who gives himself or refuses to give himself, but never lends himself. We do not hold that this is the fine flower of humanity.   We do not even want an ever increasing number of specimens.   But we know that when there are not enough of them about, immediately, the spirit of Legality gets the best of the Spirit of Justice, Obedience becomes Conformism, and the Institutions intended for the protection of individuals and families sacrifice them to the cause of their own frantic development.

Men of Europe, you have scandalised the world, but scandal there must be.   There is not much left, now, for you to lose or to take care of. In the wheels within wheels of the colossal slave-making machine, you may be that perpetually dangerous flint-dust which keeps the zeal of its technicians alive and holds in check its voracity.   Some of you are degraded : the men who in Moscow, Rome, Berlin or Madrid supplied the State police forces with their effectives—warders, spies, executioners ; and the profiteers of civil or national wars ; and also the preferment-mongering intellectuals, who toadied to the powers that be and betrayed both the Spirit and the Intellect.   But the World to-day has no right to blame us for the ignominious behaviour of these wretches, for they are the very men whom it will be treating respectfully tomorrow.   Governments always need policemen, business men and casuists ; they will enlist their services without loss of time.   Is that clear ?   Is it quite clear to you that all over the surface of the globe, the Neutral will find himself in the same camp, morally, as men who might well say this, in answer to his strictures : " Listen, we were warders, executioners, profiteers and sellers of preferment for the same reason as you were neutral—to save our skins and make some money. If we howled with the wolves instead of keeping quiet, it was because we were within reach of their fangs.   What would you have done, you hypocrites ? "   Far from damning his strayed brethren, the Neutral will politely beg them to keep quiet and not cast aspersions on the Sacred Union of Big Business, so indispensible to economic revival. Tomorrow's Peace, like yesterday's, will only come across one species of men whom it cannot swallow at all—the hero, alive or dead.

I feel some reticence in writing this much-abused word, but I can't find another.   So I will just use it in its humblest sense.   By hero, I mean anyone who has shown himself capable of heroism, and who has once—I do not say once for all, just once—put honour before life. There is no need to answer hurriedly that in given circumstances most normally endowed human beings are capable of making the less usual choice.   My answer is that nothing can be truer.   That is why war-time heroism is so ephemeral, and the war hero so disappointing. Realistic politicians rely on that, and they are not wrong to do so.   It is strictly true that to a society founded on the Profit motive, the sacrifice of life to honour is a monstrosity, for of all conceivable acts, it is the only unprofitable one.   It results from this that a realistic Society is certainly to be excused for considering the after-Victory period as one of sore trial, during which it must at any cost bring its

heroes down to its own level.   But the old political and business cynics
know that the prognosis of such a crisis is generally favourable, because
a war hero is of all heroes the most fickle and frail, once he stops
leading the life that conditioned him.   I am aware of all this ; the
experience of the last peace was enough in itself, and yet . . .   Oh !
Englishmen, for whom I began writing these pages, I am now turning
to you again.   But not only to you.   I come from too far off to speak
only to you.   For we are coming a long way back, we French ; we
really are coming from the very depth of the night ; don't expect any
of those bright messages of hope which dawn pours from the skies with
its triumphal blessing.   Mine is mere vague expectation, scarcely
ready to be put into words.   I think we shall see great things, but as
usual they will spring where they are least expected.   We need only
say *salvation* for us all to go about with our noses in the air, which is,
you must admit, an odd habit for Christians.   The Jews of Nazareth
went about with their noses in the air, and the Child Jesus was playing
in the Synagogue Square ; they bumped into Him as they passed without
even seeing Him.

Englishmen, the destitution and humiliation of men is in process of
sprouting under the soil ; and like all seed, it first of all had to rot.
Excuse this poetic language : what I mean is that the enormity of our
deception is no reason for despair, but rather a bolster for our courage.
The idealists have been deceived, but so have the realists.   The
materialist civilisation which seemed likely, in the days of Queen
Victoria, to work out indefinitely in favour of bankers and businessmen,
spares them no more than the rest of the flock.   For fifty years now,
the schemers have been as often and as harshly flouted in their scheming
as the dreamers in their illusions.   They don't admit it very readily,
because they provided our civilisation with a meaning, and it has never
seriously occurred to them that civilisation might have another meaning
which will one day come to light.   The modern world is there in front
of us like a huge piece of machinery ; and knowing what it has wasted
in money and work, we reckon what it would now cost to demolish it . . .
But civilisations are not pieces of machinery at all ; they cannot be
taken down like hangars made of steel beams ; they are alive, they
obey the laws of life.   Why should they not be re-absorbed ?   Perhaps
a tiny shift in equilibrium among such complex forces will bring us
salvation ?   Perhaps freedom will be saved by a very small number of
men—small in relation to the innumerable crowd of cowards and fools ?

As I recently reminded you English, the 1918 politicians quickly
succeeded in eliminating the Front Line men.   A few months after
the armistice, fearless lads started trembling again before the most
minor bureaucrats and humbly taking off their hats to quondam
profiteers now become millionaires.   But this first experience is not
as conclusive as the realists believe, for to-day there is a new factor to
be taken into account, which may wreck all their calculations.   Hunger-
stricken Europe is no longer at war ; it is in a state of revolution.   You

English may go on fighting without hate, as we ourselves fought twenty-five years ago, because you are meeting soldiers. The disarmed nations have masters armed to the teeth, who cannot be tackled face to face, honestly, and they must get used to killing them from behind, like dogs. You have your glorious dead; the nations of Europe have martyrs. Germany's power of domination, her ability to crush, are enormous; but the revolutionary forces taking shape in Europe are in process of countering this pressure, bit by bit. Sooner or later they will explode. That I should be glad of this may seem strange to some who know that I am a Christian. It is, however, as a Christian that I am glad. I rejoice at the thought: the universal complicity of the preferment-mongers in both the spiritual and temporal Orders has not succeeded finally in enforcing the unworthy concept of established power and of the status quo; or in substituting the fiction of Legality for the principle of Legitimacy. I am delighted that their horrible opportunism has not completely dishonoured the very name of loyalty. To obey all and sundry is to know the meaning of service no longer. To respect anyone and anything is to have lost touch with one of the noblest human virtues, veneration. When I regret that the world no longer has its share of unruly men, I am not betraying the cause of order. No leader worthy of the name has ever wanted to rule a nation of underlings; that is the idle dream of schoolteachers and altar fowls; but a man can only lean on what will stand up to him. Among so many ruins, the totalitarian demi-god has at least rendered one tremendous service to the men of Europe: they now know what a Tyrant is. In a few years' time, the word rebellion might have meant a mere intellectual attitude, usually with a megalomaniac bias. But the Tyrant of Europe is one of flesh and blood: the rebellion of Europe will be weighed down with flesh and blood too. Little by little Freedom is stripped of its juridical definitions; it is becoming human again and taking on human form, to be once more man's living helpmate. God grant that man learn how to defend her again, not as an ever-revocable privilege granted by Law, but as flesh of his flesh !

There is my message, English friends, for what it is worth. I am afraid it will seem to you an insignificant and even petty conclusion to all these pages, for the crucial importance of the events I foretell will not come to light till later on. I say that governments will not get the better of the heroes this time, for the disciplined heroes of the national war will tomorrow be joined by the insurgents of the war of Freedom. Anyhow, they won't be able to quell the ferment of revolt quickly enough: the dough will have time to rise. It is no good saying that only the moralist sees anything interesting in this—wait a while . . . Our experts keep declaring that human nature is always and everywhere the same. True enough, it does not change much; but supposing the tiniest little modification can set up incalculable repercussions ? Between freezing and boiling point, in an inorganic substance, like water, for instance, you count a hundred degrees centigrade; but a variation of only a degree or two in a living man's temperature can turn him into a dead one—do you see ? Well, man's temperature had fallen below normal ; and I say that it is rising.

While Congresses are being convened for the purpose of creating still more perfect organisations for collective security, it may seem odd that I should want to put my hope in men scattered all over Europe, separated by frontiers and by language, who have in common little more than the experience of taking risks and the habit of not yielding to threats. " Where would you lead them ? " people will ask. " I shall lead them nowhere ; I am not their leader."—" Where will they lead you ? "—I cannot say, exactly ; but I do know where your Committees of financiers, economists and medical experts will lead you. They will all pretend to be at our service, at the service of the common good ; and, consciously or not, they will be at the service of the State and work for it alone. The least attempt to better our lot will draw more heavily upon us that vast legislative and administrative apparatus, that for stupendous complexity has only been surpassed by the last of the Roman Emperors. Whether the schemes of these gentlemen are carried out or not, that portion of our Freedom that we shall have staked in the experiment will never be returned to us ; we shall have one liberty less, and the State one right more. I should not like you to think bureaucracy was an obsession of mine. When a nation turns to bureaucracy, as people say the blood of a man with dropsy turns to water, it is because it is already infected. To me, bureaucracy is merely the outward sign of the State's requirements ; and the mistake would be to believe that the State is sufficiently its own master to hold its requirements within bounds ; whereas, beyond a certain point, it can only wax, and we only wane. When our comfort and security at any price are derived from it alone, as once, at Munich, " peace at any price " from the goodwill of the dictators, why should it bother to ask us to give up our freedom of thought ? We shall probably be only too glad to hand it over, for it will no longer be really ours. Our rights will have lapsed for lack of use.

This process appears inevitable to the realistic experts, but I am not perturbed. It is logical, but not inevitable ; and the logic of realistic experts is rarely that of Nature or of History. Human society does seem to be evolving towards a sort of universal collectivism, I admit ; but this is because human defensive powers seem to be struck numb. And yet they do still exist : their reaction will be staggering. Then what is needed to set it off ? Only the passionate desire of some thousand free, proud men.

The nations which have lost their sense of Freedom will find it again only through blood and tears, in the depths of utter servitude. The capital event is this : nearly all Europe is to-day in bondage. I say *in bondage*. It is a long time since degenerate man distinguished between discipline and bondage ; they slipped from one into the other, and the world remained indifferent. Enslaved, oppressed. Not oppressed in the sense a " misunderstood " woman gives the word, or even a good French Catholic under an anti-clerical government, but down-trodden, stifled, pinned to the earth with outspread arms, the master's knees firmly planted on its chest—do you see ? Enslaved, down-trodden, humiliated, despised. They had all grown more or less used to injustice and immunised against it. But now it is fed to them in such strong doses that they must vomit or die . . . " Swallow it or die ! " says the Executioner. Those who swallow it die off even sooner than the others, or else rot alive, to the general disgust. " Swallow it or die ! "—doesn't that sound somehow familiar ? The Pagan State is finding its tongue again ; or rather it had never forgotten it ; it was we who misunderstood. " Swallow or die ! "—why not " Worship or die ! " ?

For twenty centuries, our people had not heard the command to sacrilege, the cursed word. Being the first to utter it, Germany is faithful to her historic role and spiritual vocation, which has always been to give herself away too quickly, and to compromise, through too much haste, the carrying out of the plans of Evil, revealing the hidden purpose. This is Germany's challenge to human conscience. I want this statement to stand out clearly. I do not mean by human conscience public opinion, tabulated by all the Gallup polls in the world—certainly not. Human conscience is not real except in candid and free men. In the unlikely event of only one remaining, that man would be the whole of human conscience. This is Germany's challenge : not only in her own name, but in the name of a doctrine ; and this doctrine she holds in common with all her avowed allies in Spain, Italy and France, as well as with her secret accomplices. It is a challenge in the name of a God-State, and it is not from her Teutonic ancestors that she inherited this variety of idolatry : it is from Pagan Rome. Not that ancient Rome was alone in being idolatrous ; but it passed idolatry on to us in its most serious and tenacious form. The poison still runs in our veins. The democratic élites are full of potential idolaters, waiting for the opportunity to slip from the anonymous dictatorship of Law into that of Decrees, and from that of Decrees into that of the Decree Incarnate, the omnipotent, omniscient Fuehrer. This is precisely why I do not rely on the social, intellectual or even religious élites to answer Germany's challenge ; I have put my hopes in the hands of the insurgents. I call upon the Spirit of Rebellion ; not out of blind, unreflecting hatred for Conformism, but because I would rather see the world risk its soul than deny it. This is how modern medicine treats general paralysis : by induced high fever. I do not expect the men I have in mind to organise the commonwealth of the future, the New Christendom ; I hope they will make it possible at last, by forcing the masters of consciences to answer yes or no. For that is the whole story. Our only chance lies in setting spiritual forces ablaze, whatever may kindle them.

This was Germany's challenge to Christian conscience, but the Christian conscience is Christ, and Christ answers no challenges ; it is for the Christians to do that. I have no illusions about Christians. I never believed that the Lord chose us because we are worth more than others ; and but for the absurdity of trying to penetrate the designs of Providence, I should feel inclined to believe the opposite. But if people are free not to share our beliefs, it is iniquitous of them to attribute wrong ones to us. To every Christian worthy of the name, the mystery of the Incarnation is not in the Exaltation of pious men and women and their pastors, but in the divine Humiliation. When He deigned to hide Himself among us Christians, God was not unaware —if I may say so—that He would not be recognised easily. Nothing is more natural than that unbelievers should be amazed or shocked at our laziness or paltriness. We, however, know all too well how clumsy and heavy an instrument we are in Sovereign Hands, and that for all the teaching of the Gospel, we shall always, without fail, insist on working through all the prudence and all the cunning of this world's wisdom—*Sapientia Mundi*—before making up our minds to tackle the risks of the other. Never mind. It is not a question of what *we* want and *we* can do, but of what God wants and can do for us, and that is a very different thing. When the time comes, He will post His Church against the wall, having carefully cut off every way of escape, right, left and behind ; and it will lean with its whole weight on the obstacle, with all the heroism of the Saints, as well as all the accumulated inertia of the mediocre, and then what good will it be to try to distinguish between the cowards and heroes, those who rush into the fray and those who " run away forwards " because there is no other way out ?

Naturally, I cannot blame the realistic politicians for having a realistic idea of the Church, that is, treating it as a political power like any other. If that was all it is, it would be no more than an historic memory by now, for the highly vaunted politics of the churchmen are not up to their reputation ; if you examine them closely, they are cunning and naïve both at once. Almost cynical opportunism, operating of necessity on the two planes of human prudence and divine wisdom, private interest and conscience, will get no one very far. If Church was merely a political ramp, it is incredible that, over the course of centuries, it could have taken in so many clear-seeing saints, most of whom suffered not only *for* it but *through* it ? No one doubts that the Church should be a form of government, but as such its movements are extremely slow and awkward and its inertia colossal ; almost as though God had half-paralysed its limbs in order to develop its inner life the more fully. The Church's body is infirm, and the illusion of the earth's demi-gods is easy to understand : deceived by its vast bulk, they think they need fear no other enemy ; they draw close guardedly, touch it with the very tips of their fingers, then little by little become bolder, until they think they have won the day. " So that's all it is ! " they think. They never suspect that the reactions of this great body are different from any they have experienced. It is the same kind of mistake that a Negro potentate makes, stricken with wonder at a white man submitting without protest to being deprived of his old top-hat or umbrella, while he grimly grasps in his palm a little transparent pebble, like any bit of glass, which he calls a diamond.

The body of the Church bestirs itself only when constrained by the Being Who dwells in it—ordinarily it is absorbed in contemplation and prayer, but remains amazingly sensitive to certain mysterious warnings, and to certain signs accessible to it alone—and this constraint is obviously above all hard to bear. The Body of the Church is never more ailing than when the Spirit is about to triumph. That is why the silence and the increasing embarrassment of the Pastors during the last two years, far from disturbing me, warns me that the time is at hand. Just as any of us do when God calls, they too, before obeying, try all legitimate means, not, of course, to shirk the day of trial, but at least to postpone it. What can you expect ? When so much effort has been spent in acquiring the wisdom of this world, it is hard to admit that it is all useless. When dialectics and casuistry have been practised so long, it is hard to be constrained to obey the Gospel precept, and to answer only Yes or No . . . all the harder and all the more painful because these Wise men, these Doctors, do not feel at the end of their resources or their patience at all ; each of them has in a drawer plans for a new inevitable, infallible diplomatic offensive . . . But another patience has come to an end ; though it seemed inexaustible, it is drying up suddenly, without apparent reason, for its source is elsewhere; it is the Patience of the Saints, which is probably one with the Patience and Endurance of the Poor : *Patientia pauperum non peribit in aeternum . . .*

I don't want to annoy incredulous readers by talking about the Devil, but after all journalists and heads of State are always referring to him under names like Evil, the " Forces of Evil " ; why should I be more cautious ? It seems to be generally assumed that the Devil is the Spirit of Rebellion—an opinion very warmly welcomed by the Conservatives, as it authorises them to send all the Discontented to Hell and all the Policemen to Heaven. The Devil was himself a rebel, and this I do not deny. But no proof exists that it is his plan to seduce men in the same way as he seduced the Angels. On the contrary : experience goes to show that he considers it less easy to lead us astray through the Spirit of Rebellion than to vilify us through the Spirit of Servitude, and that, far from proposing to raise us to the Satanic dignity of Rebel Angels, his clear-seeing hatred contemplates forcing us down to the level of beasts. If such an hypothesis shocks you, so much the worse. Among the few sinners—the very few— whom Christ damned in the Gospels, do you find many rebels, many disturbers of the peace ? The only ones I can find were conformists,

people bound to a faith with no generosity, and to discipline with no
love.   Love, that is the final word.   Only a free man can love.

I am not saying that Hitler is Anti-Christ.   As such, I am afraid
he must have been a disappointment to the Devil, for he has regenerated
Freedom by a new baptism, he has washed it and purified it in the blood
of the martyrs.   At that word, the Pharisees used to raise their eye-
brows and the Doctors of the Law rushed to their libraries to consult
the Dictionary of Distinctions . . .   But now it is not a matter for
speculative controversy, or negotiations intended to mollify both the
oppressor and the oppressed.   Are those who are dying, dying in vain ?
Is the good they are dying for, worth dying for ?   If the god of Europe
has not yet dared to make his servants worship him, he does openly
demand a total gift from them, and this fantastic claim already seems
quite natural to a number of fools, among them Mr. Camille Mauclair,
for instance, who announces that he is ready to divest himself of his
free will.   It is no longer pertinent to answer with pompous phrases ;
and we are indebted to Hitler now for throwing the negotiators out of
work and reducing everyone to silence.   That this silence will be
broken no one doubts.   The blood which now flows may still be the
blood of the men of good will, but that of saints will mingle with it,
and once that has happened, nothing more can shatter the solidarity
of the martyrs.

What I am saying is that an epoch in the History of the Church has
closed, the one which began with Luther's Reformation.   For all
these centuries, it seems the Church could not forget this terrible blow,
which caught it at the height of its wealth and power.   Whereas until
then it had been a thousand times more daring in its research work
and speculations than any of the monks who set themselves against it
as champions of a strict and literal interpretation of texts, it now
believed itself to be betrayed by Science.   Guardian of the highest
traditions of the Spirit, it now believed Freedom, too, had betrayed it ;
without rhyme or reason, it let itself be defied and flouted in the name
of the very principle it had firmly and once for all set upon its metaphysical foundations, for hatred of which the Roman Empire had
wanted to uproot it from the earth.   It is impossible to doubt that this
painful inferiority complex was more or less fostered, both within and
without the Church, by the institution and men who gained prestige
and profit by this means.   I repeat, this epoch is over, and another is
starting.   Incredulous readers will doubtless say that this fact—so
important to me—means nothing to them.   They must see their
mistake.   When the Church is conscious that its possessions or prestige
are threatened, it draws closer to the governments undergoing the
same trials, and attempts to link its fate with theirs.   But it would be
foolish and iniquitous to try to estimate its resources, when it is relying
on accessory values and is therefore unable to draw upon the deep,
essential forces at its disposal.   If for the incredulous reader these
forces are, a priori, of no account, that is his business.   But I fear he

is nursing many illusions as to the ones to which he pins his faith to-day. As I have repeated many times throughout these pages, it is not Society which is in the greatest peril now, but rather man, and this is how it must always have been. But such truth finds few to preach it, for the defence of Society is certainly more profitable than the defence of Man . . . In short, man is not made to live alone, and the scattered members of the flock will infallibly end by coming back to it. Whereas if man one day sacrifices the rights of the ' Person to some Collectivity he will never find them again, for that collectivity will continually grow in power and material efficiency. I know what you will say : you will tell me that the democratic community will never threaten the sacred rights of the Person. Excuse me, how can I be sure ? Why should the majority not impose its own moral code on me tomorrow, if mine is an obstacle to its profit-making ? I grant that there exists a sort of traditional democratic religion of which freedom of thought, for instance, remains an essential dogma. But a democracy without religion, provided it observes the rules of the game and abides by the decisions of universal suffrage, would still be democracy, would it not ? There are democrats and democrats, and a fifth-century Athenian would not have had much in common with Mr. Gladstone. When Mr. Roosevelt says, " I am a democrat", it amounts to saying, " I am a Christian". But ultimately, if ninety per cent of his compatriots came to hold an entirely different notion of the relationship between the Individual and the State, they would all the same continue to elect a House of Representatives, a Senate and a President. Would they not still be a democracy ?

The Free man has but one enemy, the Pagan State, whatever it may be called, whether blatant, under a tyrant, or hiding embedded in the ease and pleasure-loving masses. Against its material power we can accomplish nothing : it already controls our work and our lives. Modern economic organisation has wonderfully favoured its growth, and the enormous war effort has placed the whole machinery under its control. Of all the State has taken, we know it will return nothing, or only a shadow. But I am ashamed to talk of this god as though it had an entity, when it is no more than the horrible sum total of all our ignorance, laziness, cowardice, fear and greed. Men who want to make the group responsible for their duties or risks cannot but cede it their rights as well. Even to-day, faced with the greatest catastrophe in all history, you hardly ever hear these wretches say that tomorrow they will try and change and become better. They are not concerned with improving themselves, only the Constitution and State. Their hope is for legislation so miraculous that it will undertake to be just and reasonable on their behalf, letting them stay as they are and grow wealthy and have a good time not only without risk but without remorse either. They will continue to wax fat at the expense of the poor devils, but the State will take care of the poor devils they have ruined in its institutions. They will beget children, but the State will pay for the pregnancy, pay for the confinement, pay for the nurse, subsidise the brat and decorate its parents. Or else they will refuse to procreate and the State will pay others to do the job for them. They will cut down trees, dry up wells, poison rivers, but the Community will assume the cost of afforestation, and build reservoirs and huge hatcheries for the artificial insemination of fish. In short they could practise all the vices and the State would protect them from the consequences ; in their frenzy for profit-making, they would lay waste all the riches of the earth, and in return for a small levy on their dividends, that Magician the State would re-establish these riches at the end of every quarter ; in such circumstances, it would be as difficult to hold up the State in its soaring career towards omnipotence as it would be to stop these craven creatures in their stampede towards slavery, for I repeat, the two phenomena are but one. But at least we can refuse to bend the knee and sacrifice to the gods of the City, as our ancestors did two thousand years ago. The totalitarian Masters are obviously conscious of the overshadowing Roman Empire, and in their parvenu eagerness, they are all too zealous in making sure no one remains unaware of what Order it is of which they are legitimate heirs.

True, for a long time now Christians and their Pastors have realised that the Modern State and the New Order are not so new as they make out : but they are too polite to ask to see their birth certificate, and too much afraid that Nero or Domitian may have signed it as witnesses at the Registry office ... Hitler, however, is very fond of pushing this document under their noses, and even rubs their faces in it, for he is a lad who in his youth was better acquainted with doss-houses than Embassy drawing-rooms, and he has disconcerting manners. Never mind. The time is not far off when the most obstinate optimists will have to yield to evidence. What sort of evidence ? Streams of innocent blood. Chancellries have not very sensitive olfactory organs and, like Juvenal's courtesans, no filth can make them vomit. But the smell of innocent blood numbs them and keeps them quiet.

Free men, who are dying at this instant and whose names even we do not know ; free men, dying alone at dawn between glaring bare walls ; free men, dying friendless with no priests, sweet familiar home-scenes in your mind's eye ; free men, who as you cross the short space between your prison and the ditch, feel on your shoulders the sweat of a night of agony grow chilly ; free men, dying with undaunted words on your lips, and those who die weeping—wondering bitterly if it is all for nothing—the sigh from your bullet-shredded lungs rises unheard, but this slight breath is the breath of the Spirit. I am not using the language of a pulpit orator or a neo-Catholic poet ; I am stating a true fact, as simple as two and two make four. Free men, many of you would be most surprised to learn that you are marching in the vanguard of Christianity, that God hurls you forward to open the breach. And if I told you so to your very faces, you might answer with blasphemies, for you see the word Christian as an equivocal word, used to establish and justify all forms of bondage, from complacency to complicity, from treason and perjury to cowardly submission. We know that such Christians exist, we know they thrive and prosper in the Church till the day comes when, confident in their final success, they lose all.

Nor is that a bit of rhetoric either ! For the Gospel drama is repeated century after century, with marvellous precision. God does not choose the same men to keep His Word or to fulfill it. If all the pious would only observe these necessary distinctions, they would understand the history of the Church much better ; they would stop being surprised and would rejoice at the silence of the doctors and casuists, for when these mighty personages talk too loud, conscience is no longer heard ; the text itself is smothered under commentaries. The important thing is not whether the Scribes define Christian Man one way or another, in order to reassure Caesar and postpone the moment for decisive explanations as long as possible. What does matter is to know exactly what Christian Man is. For there is a type of Christian Man, and that type is consecrated by the Church itself ; it is the Saint. The Saints are the Army of the Church. Do we judge the strength of a nation by the quality of its diplomats ? Well, Church-diplomats aren't much good ; and precisely because they are mediocre, they cling obstinately to their jobs ; they are like clumsy acrobats always starting off afresh. But the Church in arms—that's what counts—and I'm not talking about artillery or machine guns.

The Church in arms—that means the Church on foot, with the Saints in front. It is true that the Church only rises at the last moment —which amounts to saying that it only fights with its back to the wall, when it has become impossible to move back a single inch, because it would lose then at one fell stroke both Spiritual and Temporal, Appearance and Reality, Virtue and Status, Heaven and Earth. Do you see ? When the spirit of Munich gets hold of the democracies, I haven't the least idea how far they would let panic carry them ; whereas History shows me the precise point at which, come what may, the Church will have to make a stand. For it can let the bond which binds it to the Saints grow slack, but it cannot let it be severed or the penalty is death. You may suppose the Saints to be as ridiculous as you like, but let me tell you that the Masters of the World can find no tougher nut to crack. They are people who render unto Caesar what belongs to Caesar, but who would let themselves be made into mincemeat before giving him more than his due. Yet it is exactly what does not belong to him that Caesar most wants. But he is very careful not to say so at first, and these chaps don't let themselves be drawn into arguments and compromises ; they quietly and firmly place in the outstretched hand of the State what is owing to it, they may add a small tip, to make it even ; and then it is over and done with. For nothing Caesar possesses could possibly arouse their envy. And I say that this courteous indifference is a thousand times more galling a retort to Caesar's claims than all the insults and threats of the anarchists, because it is terribly catching, and is both an object of emulation for noble souls and the hope and consolation of the downtrodden. It would be a mistake for you to suppose I mean only the calendar Saints ! There are millions of Saints in the world, known only to God, and who certainly do not deserve to be raised to the altars—a very inferior and rustic breed of saint, saints of very humble origin, with only one drop of sainthood in their veins, and who are as much like real saints as a gutter-cat is like a prize Persian or Siamese. Usually there is nothing special to distinguish them from the mass of ordinary good folk ; nor are they conscious of being different ; and the Church itself takes care not to undeceive them, at least while it is bargaining with Caesar. It boasts to him of their obedience, their respect for established laws, their harmless lives ; it does not mind their being taken for chumps : what is the good of disclosing them too soon ? It knows they exist and that they outlive all scandals, all treason, all promotion-buying ; and that their species, tough as gutter-cats, will suddenly and prodigiously multiply the moment it dares to speak their language, the moment the blood of the martyrs wells. They have already once overturned the Pagan State. Now did they, or did they not ? Though we don't refuse to take the " Render unto Caesar that which is Caesar's " in a very broad sense ; and we are willing to interpret the words of the *Magnificat* in a way not too disturbing to the Powerful ; and we never said the early Christians were rebels in the theological sense : we must ask you to realise that that is what they certainly seemed to be to the Empire, and to the Empire's bureaucracy, and to all the Empire's traditionalist and moderate way of thinking. I can't help it. However anxious one may be not to fall from one extreme into the other, it does grate on one to hear good, plump canons talking of the Sermon on the Mount as though it were a conservative manifesto. One gets the impression that this distinguished company would not care to be reminded, at the end of an official dinner for instance, that the first twenty-two Popes were judged, condemned and executed as disturbers of Order. When an Institution, even the most respectful to the powers that be, numbers among its founders such a series of condemned criminals, it seems difficult to presume that it will always find favour with professors of Law and Civic Morality, and landlords, bailiffs and police . . . To-day, like twenty centuries ago, it is all a matter of whether Justice according to Order, or Order according to Justice, will come out on top.

For there is the knot of the argument. We all talk about Justice, but we are not all thinking of the same Justice. Mine is that of the Gospels, and I admit it must seem singularly paradoxical to the Professors of Law, Political Economy and Physiology. It is on this paradox that our freedom is founded. Christianity even makes man holy. And nothing less than this fact will counterbalance, to some extent, the enormous advantage which the community enjoys over the Individual. The man who relies solely on human Order will sooner or later fall under the iron law of the mammoth City. To expect the coming of the Kingdom of Man alone is to be deprived in due course of the Kingdom of God, that is, of Justice, for the triumph of man in this world can be achieved only through ruthless discipline ; we shall enter the Earthly Paradise only by trampling the Poor, Weak and Infirm, the very ones extólled in the Gospel of the Beatitudes. And then, too late, it will be realised that the totalitarian régimes covered the same ground, in a few years only, as the realist and materialist democracies were to cover in a century or two. It is more than likely that when I talk like this, the intellectual élites just laugh. I don't mind if they do. Let me tell them that they are not through with the demi-gods, and I may live long enough to see them, once more, crouching at the feet of the Masters. There is no need for them to insult me by supposing me guilty of some monstrous vision of clerical domination ! I have never imagined that Christianity was to become actual in so crude a form. We expect of the Church what God Himself expects : the training of really free men, a particularly effective kind of free men, because freedom is for them not only a right, but an obligation, a duty, for which they account to God. I cannot help it if you think I am splitting hairs. We shall come back to the subject when the human herds, surfeited, stuffed, filled to bursting, shall bless their bondage and remember their souls as a cynical old man remembers his early loves. The word freedom will not of course be struck out of the dictionary, but there will be no lack of sophists to prove that, once the Community has settled this matter of Good and Evil, the man who obeys is free, the slave is he who resists. Good God, these are theories we know quite well ! They rallied the masses of German democracy to nazism. Coming from what pen, uttered by what lips, will they reappear tomorrow ?

You expect large returns from freedom. All I hope for is honour. Even though it brought me, as a Christian, all sorts of harm, the honour it bestows would still be dearer than life itself, because it is the honour of the God I serve, Who wishes to be served by free men. There is no point in saying that this metaphysical freedom is of no interest to the Community, and that it is only too glad to leave it to me. For sooner or later it will ask for it in the name of public welfare, Economics, Science or something else. It will ask for it because, through the increasingly greater means at its disposal, its old, old dream of a gregarious civilisation will finally reach its paroxysm ; because we shall never enter its hives and shall never recognise, without all-important reservations, the biological law of the species. We have no illusions as to our strength, of course ; we quite understand the proud parade of the élite before our plain service-men : they hardly know we exist, and we don't of course play our full part, modest though it is, except in crucial circumstances of a kind which the Wise call desperate.

Desperate indeed, but only for them ! For the despair of the Wise is full to overflowing with promise and hope, as far as we are concerned ! It is the signal that the Enemy of the world has crossed the lines, that the defences which we were not allowed to touch, because they were not ours, have been broken and overrun. The battle which we were forbidden to incite is now before us. I must apologise for using these belligerent metaphors, just like any preacher trying to rouse the zeal of pious women ; but it is not my fault. However incredible it may seem, it is the plain truth that as Christians we hold ourselves responsible —and alone responsible—for human freedom, because we are responsible before God. Not, mark you, for the Rights of Man, but for the principle of legitimacy in which they are founded. You have no great liking for principles, I know ; you use signs instead ; but a time comes when these signs have no more worth than banknotes at the end of a period of inflation. The Kings of France were powerful lords from the twelfth century, yet what was left to Charles the Dauphin in 1429 ? Neither Judges, nor Men-at-arms, nor Clerics could possibly give back to him what he had lost. But with her quiet good sense, the wise child of Lorraine knew exactly what had to be done first : against the will of the Churchmen even, she insisted that first of all they were to make this young prince a Consecrated King. When man has lost everything, we, too, shall insist on his being annointed, whatever happens, so that he may be made holy ; we shall work till there is no obstacle left between him and his Consecration.